The Hidden Weight
Of Fat-Belly Shame

Finding Strength, Freedom, And Faith Beyond The Mirror

By Minister Joyce Toney

Published by **GOD'S DESIGN4YOU INC / YESICAN Ministries**

Scripture quotations are taken from the Amplified Bible, unless otherwise noted.

ISBN: 978-0-9792821-3-3

Printed in the United States of America.

Contact: bhbp@yesican77.com

Website: www.yesican77.com

TABLE OF CONTENTS

Dedication....1

Acknowledgments....2

Introduction....3

Understanding The Hidden Weight Of Shame....3

Chapter 1: The Mirror Doesn't Lie — But It Doesn't Tell The Truth Either....5

Chapter 2: The Voice Behind The Mirror....11

Chapter 3: "The Shame Syndrome....17

Chapter 4: "Inherited Lies And Learned Comparisons" Part One....23

Chapter 4: "Inherited Lies And Learned Comparisons" Part Two....27

Chapter 5: "The Burden Beneath The Belly." Part One....30

Chapter 5: "The Burden Beneath The Belly." Part Two....34

Chapter 6: When The Heart Feels Heavy – Part One....39

Chapter 6: When The Heart Feels Heavy – Part -Two....43

Chapter 7: Breaking The Curse Of Condemnation-Part-1....48

Chapter 7: Breaking The Curse Of Condemnation-Part-2....53

Chapter 8: The Mirror Of Mercy -Part 1....58

Chapter 8: The Mirror Of Mercy -Part 2....63

Chapter 9: "The Language Of Healing - Part One....68

Chapter 9: The Language Of Healing – Part Two....73

Chapter 10: The Spirit Of Restoration – Part Two....79

Chapter 10: The Spirit Of Restoration – Part One....85

Chapter 11: Breaking Emotional Agreements With Shame – Part One 90

Chapter 11: Breaking Emotional Agreements With Shame – Part Two 96

Chapter 12: The Weight Of Words Unspoken – Part One 102

Chapter 12: The Weight Of Words Unspoken – Part Two 107

Chapter 13: Reclaiming The Temple Within – Part One.................................... 113

Chapter 13: Reclaiming The Temple Within – Part Two................................... 118

Chapter 14: Learning To Live Light: The Freedom Of Release – Part One 124

Chapter 14: Learning To Live Light: The Freedom Of Release – Part Two 128

Chapter 15: When God Redefines Beauty – Part One 134

Chapter 15: When God Redefines Beauty – Part Two 139

Chapter 16: The Benediction Of Becoming (Part One & Part Two).............. 145

Chapter 16: Part Two – The Healing Light Of The Heart.................................... 148

DEDICATION

To every heart that has stood before the mirror and struggled to see God's beauty within—to those who have been wounded by comparison, criticism, and cultural judgment, yet still long to walk free.

This book is dedicated to you—the warriors of faith who rise from the shadows of shame to reflect the light of Kingdom confidence.

May you discover the unshakable truth that your body, soul, and spirit were designed by God for His glory, not for the world's approval.

ACKNOWLEDGMENTS

With deep gratitude to the Lord Jesus Christ, whose love covers all shame and whose truth renews every soul. This work exists because of His grace and guidance. To the mentors, intercessors, and faith partners of God Design4You / YESICAN Ministries, thank you for standing with me in prayer and purpose. Your support turns vision into reality.

To those who have walked through the journey of self-rejection and now stand redeemed—your testimonies inspired these pages.

You are living proof that the weight of shame cannot stand against the power of God's love.

And to my family in faith, who believed when the burden felt too heavy—thank you for reminding me that grace always wins.

INTRODUCTION

UNDERSTANDING THE HIDDEN WEIGHT OF SHAME

Shame is not just an emotion; it is a spiritual chain that seeks to disconnect the soul from its divine identity.It whispers lies that say, "You are not enough," and feeds the illusion that worth is measured by outward perfection. From a spiritual perspective, shame is the inner distortion of truth. It began when humanity first hid from God, as Adam and Eve did after their disobedience. Their first response to sin was not hunger or fear, but covering and hiding.

That instinct to hide reveals the true nature of shame—it is separation from spiritual alignment, a shadow that convinces us to conceal what God longs to heal.

In modern life, "fat-belly shame" has become one of the most visible expressions of this inner bondage.

It is not merely about the size of a waistline, but about the weight of worthlessness that society attaches to imperfection.

It is the ache that says, "I must shrink to be accepted," instead of, "I was created with divine purpose."

The Bible reveals that shame is never God's instrument.

While conviction draws us toward repentance, shame pushes us away from restoration.

Conviction whispers, “Come home.” Shame hisses, “You’re too far gone.”

But the heart of the Kingdom calls us back to truth:

“Those who look to Him are radiant; their faces are never covered with shame.” — Psalm 34:5

God’s desire is not to erase the body but to restore the image—the reflection of Himself within us.

When the soul is healed, the mirror changes, because the spirit begins to see through eyes of grace, not judgment.

This book is a journey through that transformation—from hiding to healing, from shame to strength.Each chapter will uncover a hidden layer of the weight we carry, both emotionally and spiritually, and replace it with Kingdom truth, freedom, and faith.

May every reader come to declare, with conviction and joy: “I am fearfully and wonderfully made. I am free. I am whole. I am His.”

CHAPTER 1

THE MIRROR DOESN'T LIE — BUT IT DOESN'T TELL THE TRUTH EITHER

Theme & Focus

Learning to see beyond surface reflections to the divine image within. The mirror shows what time and experience have shaped, but it cannot reveal what grace has restored. This chapter invites the reader to confront distorted self-perception, replace judgment with revelation, and rediscover worth through the eyes of God.

Core Narrative (Teaching + Reflective Story Flow)

The morning light crept across the small bedroom as YesICan stood before her mirror.

She had learned to glance quickly, never to linger. Each reflection seemed to speak a language of accusation—rounded belly, tired eyes, evidence of a battle between who she was and who she longed to be.

The world had trained her to measure value in inches and numbers, in "before-and-after" pictures that whispered, *You're still not enough.* Yet somewhere deep within, another voice—quiet but steady—said, *Look again. I see more.*

That whisper was the invitation of the Spirit.

When we stare into the mirror, we see layers: the reflection that culture interprets, the story our experiences retell, and the truth Heaven still declares. The physical mirror captures the visible, but the spiritual mirror—God's Word—reveals the eternal.

YesICan's reflection was not wrong; it simply wasn't complete. It showed the shell of her story, not the substance of her spirit. Her belly carried the memories of comfort eating through seasons of grief, pregnancies that birthed both life and loss, and years of stress stored in hidden places. Yet within that same body lived resilience, purpose, and power.

She had survived much—but shame had attached itself like a silent weight. Every look in the mirror revived an inner courtroom: prosecutor, judge, and jury, all whispering the same verdict—guilty of imperfection.

But that day was different.

As she stood in the stillness, a verse came alive in her heart:

"I am fearfully and wonderfully made; marvelous are Your works." — *Psalm 139:14*

Tears blurred her reflection, but they also softened her focus. For the first time, she realized the mirror had only ever told half the truth. It showed the vessel, but not the treasure inside. It reflected her body, but not her becoming.

Every believer faces this dual reality: what the mirror shows versus what God sees. The mirror measures progress by sight; God measures transformation by surrender.

Shame thrives on the visible; grace reigns in the invisible.

Kingdom Insight

In the Kingdom, identity is not created by appearance—it is revealed through communion. When Adam and Eve hid from God after sin, their first act was to cover what they suddenly perceived as flawed. That instinct to hide birthed shame—the spiritual separation between creation and Creator.

Shame is not about fat, form, or failure. It is the false narrative that says, *I must hide because I'm unworthy of being seen.* The enemy of your soul wants to keep you gazing into distorted mirrors—mirrors of comparison, criticism, and cultural expectation—until you forget the reflection of Heaven within you.

But the Kingdom mirror reflects differently. It speaks what God spoke over David when others saw only a shepherd boy:

"The Lord does not look at the things people look at. People look at the outward appearance, but the Lord looks at the heart."
— *1 Samuel 16:7*

The true battle is spiritual. Shame blinds us to divine purpose and silences Kingdom confidence. Yet when revelation enters, the mirror becomes an altar instead of a judge. What once condemned now confirms: *You are still chosen, still loved, still called.*

Spiritual Application

To overcome "fat-belly shame," we must retrain our inner vision. Transformation begins not with the mirror on the wall but with the mirror of the Word.

Every time you stand before your reflection, speak what Heaven says:

I am God's design. My body carries His story. My scars are testimonies, not flaws.

Invite the Holy Spirit to show you what He sees. Ask Him to uncover the hidden weight—not the physical pounds, but the emotional heaviness that clings to self-judgment, fear, and rejection. Release each one into His hands.

When you choose to look through divine perspective, the mirror becomes a ministry moment. It's no longer a place of shame—it's a classroom of self-revelation.

End-of-Chapter Framework

Self-Reflection Questions

1. What emotions arise when you look at yourself in the mirror?
2. Which voices (from culture, family, or self-talk) have shaped how you define beauty or worth?
3. How might God's truth rewrite those definitions?
4. What part of your body or story have you hidden out of shame, and what would restoration look like there?

Devotional Insight

(Redirected

- **Readjusted**
- **Set Aright**
- **Increased in Holiness)**
- **Redirected:** From outward measurement to inward alignment.

- **Readjusted:** From comparing bodies to honoring God's design.
- **Set Aright:** By declaring that the temple is holy regardless of size or shape.
- **Increased in Holiness:** As the heart reflects gratitude rather than self-criticism.

Affirmation of Faith

I am fearfully and wonderfully made.

The mirror reflects only a fraction of who I am.

My true image is shaped by grace, framed in purpose, and filled with the glory of God.

I choose to see myself as Heaven sees me—whole, worthy, and radiant.

Prayer of Release / Activation

Heavenly Father,

thank You for crafting me with care and intention. Today I surrender the distorted images I've believed about myself.

Break every agreement I've made with shame and comparison.

Teach me to honor this body as Your temple and to celebrate the reflection of Your creativity within me.

Let every glance in the mirror become a moment of worship, a reminder that I am Your workmanship—fearfully and wonderfully made.

In Jesus' name, Amen.

Scripture Anchors

- **Psalm 139:14** — "I am fearfully and wonderfully made; marvelous are Your works, and that my soul knows very well."
- **1 Samuel 16:7** — "The Lord does not look at the outward appearance, but the Lord looks at the heart."

Key Takeaways

- The physical mirror can't reveal spiritual truth.
- Shame begins with hiding; healing begins with unveiling.
- God measures transformation by surrender, not by size.
- Your body is not a punishment; it is a vessel of purpose.
- Seeing through Kingdom eyes replaces condemnation with confidence.

Call to Action

Stand before a mirror today.

Instead of critiquing, *prophesy*—speak one truth from Scripture over your reflection.

Write it on a sticky note and place it where you'll see it daily.

Each declaration weakens shame's voice and strengthens your Kingdom confidence.

Remember: the mirror doesn't lie—but it doesn't tell the whole truth until you invite God's Word into the reflection.

CHAPTER 2

THE VOICE BEHIND THE MIRROR

Theme & Focus

Recognizing and silencing the voices—both inner and outer—that distort your perception of worth. This chapter reveals how shame speaks through culture, comparison, and self-condemnation, and how the Spirit restores your hearing to discern the true voice of God.

Core Narrative (Teaching + Reflective Story Flow)

There are mornings when the silence feels louder than any sound.

YesICan sat on the edge of her bed, staring at the mirror across the room. The glass held no power by itself, yet every time she looked, she heard echoes—old words, sharp and familiar:

"You've let yourself go."

"If you were more disciplined..."

"You'd be beautiful if you just lost the belly."

None of these words came from her lips, but they had found a home in her mind. They were the voices of childhood teasing, of unkind relatives, of television screens whispering perfection as a standard of holiness.

The voice behind the mirror was never just hers.

When the serpent spoke to Eve in the garden, he did not shout; he suggested. His voice created doubt—"Did God really say?"—and shifted Eve's focus from divine assurance to self-evaluation. That is how shame still works: it attaches to the power of suggestion, twisting perception until truth sounds like a lie and lies feel familiar.

YesICan realized that most of her self-criticism wasn't spontaneous—it was learned dialogue. Every insult she had absorbed had become a recording that played automatically whenever she tried to love herself.

But that morning, she decided to confront it.

She stood before the mirror and said aloud, "I hear you—but you don't speak for me anymore."

At that moment, her reflection didn't change, but her authority did. The voice that once accused began to lose its grip because truth was rising to the surface.

Kingdom Insight

Shame often disguises itself as motivation, but its true agenda is control. The enemy knows that if he can dominate your inner dialogue, he can limit your outer purpose.

Revelation 12:10 calls him "the accuser of the brethren." He speaks condemnation to separate you from confidence in God. His language is filled with "not enoughs"—not thin enough, not spiritual enough, not worthy enough.

The Spirit of God, by contrast, never accuses; He convicts with compassion, leading you toward repentance and restoration, never humiliation.

"My sheep hear My voice, and I know them, and they follow Me." —*John 10:27*

Every believer must learn voice recognition in the Spirit. When a thought produces fear, guilt, or self-hatred, it is not the Shepherd's voice. When a word produces peace, alignment, and renewed identity, that is the voice of the One who formed you.

The voice behind the mirror is not always demonic—it can also be cultural. Media amplifies the illusion that worth is earned through aesthetics. Society rewards what it sees, while the Kingdom celebrates what it reflects—the character of Christ.

To overcome fat-belly shame, we must exchange the language of criticism for the language of creation. God never called your body a mistake; He called it a temple. He never designed the stomach to be an idol or an enemy—it is part of the vessel through which His Spirit operates.

Spiritual Application

Healing begins when you confront, not comply. You cannot silence what you still agree with.

Write down the phrases you've heard about your body—spoken by others or whispered within—and bring them before God. Ask, "Father, is this what You say about me?"

Then open His Word and find the divine response. For every accusation, there is a counter-declaration:

- "You're not enough." → *"I am complete in Him."* (Colossians 2:10)

- "You should be ashamed." → *"There is now no condemnation."* (Romans 8:1)
- "You'll never change." → *"I am being transformed by the renewing of my mind."* (Romans 12:2)

As these truths take root, the inner critic grows silent. The mirror no longer echoes lies—it becomes a witness to transformation.

End-of-Chapter Framework

Self-Reflection Questions

1. What recurring words or phrases do you hear when you look at yourself?
2. Who originally spoke those words into your life?
3. How do those voices compare to what God declares in His Word?
4. What new declaration of truth will you begin speaking daily?

Devotional Insight

(**Redirected**

- **Readjusted**
- **Set Aright**
- **Increased in Holiness**)
- **Redirected:** From hearing accusation to discerning revelation.
- **Readjusted:** From rehearsing cultural lies to rehearsing Kingdom truth.

- **Set Aright:** By aligning self-talk with the language of grace.
- **Increased in Holiness:** As the heart becomes a sanctuary where only God's voice is welcome.

Affirmation of Faith

I no longer agree with the voice of shame.

I recognize the Shepherd's voice, and His words shape my identity.

My worth is not negotiable—it is established in Heaven.

I am loved, chosen, and free.

Prayer of Release / Activation

Father,

thank You for giving me ears to hear the truth above the noise.

Silence every voice that speaks contrary to Your Word.

Uproot the seeds of criticism and comparison that have grown in my soul.

Let Your Spirit teach me to recognize Your tone—gentle, patient, empowering.

From this day forward, may every reflection echo Your affirmation:

"You are Mine."

In Jesus' name, Amen.

Scripture Anchors

- **John 10:27** — "My sheep hear My voice, and I know them, and they follow Me."
- **Romans 8:1** — "Therefore, there is now no condemnation for those who are in Christ Jesus."

Key Takeaways

- Shame speaks through familiar voices; truth speaks through love.
- The enemy accuses to separate you from purpose.
- God's voice restores identity and peace.
- You have authority to reject false narratives.
- The mirror can become a place of prophecy instead of punishment.

Call to Action

Spend five minutes each morning listening in stillness before you speak.

Ask, "Lord, what do You say about me today?"

Write down one word or phrase that rises in your spirit.

Post it where you prepare for your day.

Let that divine affirmation be louder than every echo of shame.

CHAPTER 3

"THE SHAME SYNDROME

Theme & Focus

Shame Syndrome: Understanding and Breaking the Cycle

Shame is more than a fleeting emotion; it is a spiritual condition that attaches itself to identity. It convinces the heart that failure is final and that flaws mean unworthiness. This chapter exposes the inner workings of shame—the hidden system that keeps people bound to self-rejection—and reveals how God's truth interrupts that cycle with restoration and freedom.

The Anatomy of Shame

Shame operates like a syndrome—a repeating pattern of symptoms that feed one another.

It begins with **exposure**—a moment when weakness, imperfection, or vulnerability is seen.

Exposure is followed by **interpretation**—the mind translates what happened into a verdict: *I'm not enough.*

Then comes **agreement**—the soul accepts that verdict as truth.

Finally, **bondage**—life starts revolving around covering, performing, or pretending.

The longer these four stages repeat, the more normal they feel. Shame becomes a rhythm, not just a reaction.

You can see this pattern in Scripture.

After Adam and Eve sinned, "their eyes were opened," and they saw their nakedness—**exposure**.

They hid among the trees—**interpretation and agreement**—believing they could no longer stand uncovered before God.

When God called, "Where are you?" their answer revealed **bondage**: *I was afraid because I was naked, so I hid.*

This is the original shame syndrome—seeing oneself outside of grace.

How Shame Shapes the Body and Mind

Shame does not stay in the spirit; it manifests through behavior and even posture.

It lowers the eyes, curls the shoulders, and quiets the voice. It teaches the body to apologize for existing.

Modern culture amplifies this effect. Advertisements and social media praise perfection while quietly condemning imperfection. The "fat-belly" narrative tells people that visible softness equals internal weakness. Many begin living as projects to fix instead of temples to honor.

But the Lord never created you to live under a repair order. He created you to reflect His image, not someone else's approval.
The body becomes sick when the soul is silenced. Freedom begins when you stop apologizing for the space you occupy.

The Spiritual Root of the Syndrome

At its core, shame is agreement with accusation.

Revelation 12:10 calls the adversary "the accuser of the brethren."

He cannot remove salvation, so he attacks perception.

If he can make you doubt your worth, he can mute your witness.

The enemy's favorite lie is subtle: *"You should be further along by now."*

He measures holiness by progress charts, but God measures holiness by surrender.

When shame speaks, it points backward. When grace speaks, it pulls forward.

Romans 8:1 declares, "There is therefore now no condemnation for those who are in Christ Jesus."

Condemnation says, *stay hidden.* Conviction says, *come home.*

Breaking the Cycle

1. **Recognize the Pattern** – Identify where shame repeats itself: body image, family history, finances, or faith.
2. **Refuse Agreement** – Speak truth aloud: *I no longer partner with condemnation.*
3. **Replace the Voice** – Fill your mind with the Word until a new language forms inside you.
4. **Return to Relationship** – Let God's presence replace performance.

Freedom is not forgetting what happened; it is remembering who you are in spite of it.

The cross of Christ did not erase your story—it redeemed it.

Kingdom Insight

Shame thrives in secrecy, but it dies in light.

When you expose shame to truth, it cannot survive.

The Kingdom way is transparency before God—honest prayer, honest reflection, honest grace.

Isaiah 61:7 promises, "Instead of your shame you shall have double honor; instead of confusion they shall rejoice in their portion."

Double honor does not mean denial of the past; it means divine exchange—what was once disgrace becomes a display of glory. God turns what humiliated you into what illuminates His presence.

The "fat-belly" shame that society mocks is often the very place where compassion and empathy are born.

What once symbolized imperfection can become an altar of understanding—a place where you minister to others still hiding behind their own coverings.

Spiritual Application

Ask the Holy Spirit to reveal where shame has built a home. Write down the patterns—words, memories, or experiences that trigger feelings of unworthiness.

Next to each, write a counter-truth from Scripture.

Examples:

- *Lie:* "I am too far gone."

Truth: "His mercy is new every morning." (Lamentations 3:22–23)

- *Lie:* "My body disqualifies me."

Truth: "My body is a temple of the Holy Spirit." (1 Corinthians 6:19)

Then pray this simple surrender:

"Lord, I release every agreement I've made with shame. Replace every lie with Your Word. Teach me to walk in the rhythm of grace."

Repeat it daily until peace feels natural again.

Closing Reflection

Shame is not humility; it is hostility toward your own creation.

Humility acknowledges weakness and invites grace. Shame worships weakness and rejects grace.

Humility kneels to be lifted; shame hides to stay small.

The shame syndrome breaks when you remember who authored your story.

You are not the mistake—you are the miracle He chose to redeem.

Key Scriptures

- **Romans 8:1** – "There is therefore now no condemnation for those who are in Christ Jesus."

- **Isaiah 61:7** – "Instead of your shame you shall have double honor."
- **1 Corinthians 6:19** – "Your body is a temple of the Holy Spirit."

Summary of Truths

- Shame follows a cycle: exposure → interpretation → agreement → bondage.
- God interrupts the cycle through light and love.
- The body is not the enemy; it is evidence of divine craftsmanship.
- Honor replaces humiliation when truth is allowed to speak.
- Freedom begins where agreement with accusation ends.

CHAPTER 4

"INHERITED LIES AND LEARNED COMPARISONS" PART ONE

Theme & Focus

Every generation passes down spoken truths—and silent lies. Some teach us faith and endurance; others teach us to doubt our value. This chapter explores how cultural messages, family patterns, and worldly standards shape our sense of worth, and how Kingdom truth uproots those inherited distortions.

The Weight of Words Passed Down

Shame often begins before we can speak it.

Many of us were shaped by phrases whispered through generations:

"You must always look your best."

"Don't eat too much; people will talk."

"Respectable women keep themselves small."

These words sounded like guidance but carried a quiet poison. They planted seeds of conditional acceptance—teaching that approval depends on appearance, performance, or control.

Every family, culture, or community builds its own mirror. Some polish it with pride, others with perfectionism, but few teach reflection through grace. Those mirrors become our first teachers of comparison.

The lie is subtle yet powerful: to belong, you must fit.

But Kingdom identity says the opposite: to belong, you must be born again.

Generational Scripts

Inherited shame operates like an unseen script written in the subconscious.

You may never have been told you were unworthy, yet you behave as if you are constantly auditioning for love.

Consider how the Israelites carried Egypt in their minds long after they left it. God delivered them physically, but their thinking still bowed to the memory of bondage. In the same way, we can live redeemed yet still respond to life through the filters of family fear or societal pressure.

Some families pass down faith; others pass down fatigue—trying endlessly to prove they are enough. This fatigue often shows up as dieting, overworking, or comparing, all rooted in an unspoken family motto: *We must earn our dignity.*

But Kingdom truth rewrites that script:

"You are accepted in the Beloved." — Ephesians 1:6

The Culture of Comparison

Comparison is the language of a world that has forgotten its Maker.

It whispers that success has a single silhouette.

It invites us to measure joy by visibility and worth by waistline.

Social media magnifies this deception. Every scroll becomes a sermon of scarcity: *Someone else is prettier, fitter, holier, happier.*

The danger is not just envy—it's identity theft.

When you compare, you subconsciously declare that God made a mistake in designing you.

Yet Scripture says,

"We are His workmanship, created in Christ Jesus for good works." — Ephesians 2:10

You were not mass-produced; you were master-crafted.

Your difference is not a deficiency—it is divine intention.

Kingdom Insight

Inherited lies lose power when you identify their source. Not every voice from your past was malicious; many were simply misinformed. They repeated what was once spoken to them. That's why redemption includes the renewing of the mind (Romans 12:2).

To renew means to re-author.

The Holy Spirit becomes your editor, striking through the sentences of shame and writing in the language of truth.

You are not bound to repeat what you inherited—you are anointed to redeem it.

God doesn't erase family lines; He redeems them.

When you accept Kingdom identity, you become the interruption in the bloodline of comparison. You become the one who says:

"The cycle ends with me. From this point forward, the only inheritance my children receive is truth."

Spiritual Application

1. **Identify the Lie:** What belief about beauty, success, or holiness have you accepted without question?
2. **Trace the Source:** Did it come from God's Word or human opinion?
3. **Replace the Narrative:** Find Scripture that contradicts the lie and speak it daily.

Example:

- *Lie:* "Thin equals worthy."
- *Truth:* "I am fearfully and wonderfully made." (Psalm 139:14)

Each declaration shifts spiritual weight. Every time you speak truth aloud, you dismantle an inherited stronghold.

CHAPTER 4

"INHERITED LIES AND LEARNED COMPARISONS" PART TWO

Breaking the Cycle of Comparison

Comparison thrives on discontent; gratitude starves it.The more you thank God for what He has made, the less room envy has to live.Make it a daily practice to bless others without belittling yourself. When you see someone thriving, remind your heart, "Their success is proof that God is still moving in the neighborhood."

Honor does not reduce your blessing—it multiplies it.

Restoring Kingdom Vision

To heal from comparison, you must learn to see as Heaven sees.Heaven's perspective is wide and full—it sees purpose beyond size, color, or ability.

When Samuel looked at Jesse's sons, he assumed the tallest and strongest must be chosen. But God corrected him:

"Man looks at the outward appearance, but the Lord looks at the heart." — *1 Samuel 16:7*

That same truth still stands today. God never consults a mirror before calling a person.

Closing Reflection

What you inherit can either define you or refine you.

The choice lies in your agreement.

Refuse to carry forward the weight of generational comparison.

Choose instead to carry the cross of transformation—the only weight that leads to resurrection.

God is rewriting your lineage through you.

Every lie you reject becomes a door your descendants will never have to walk through.

You are not the continuation of the old story; you are the beginning of a redeemed one.

Key Scriptures

- *Ephesians 1:6* — "You are accepted in the Beloved."
- *Romans 12:2* — "Be transformed by the renewing of your mind."
- *1 Samuel 16:7* — "The Lord looks at the heart."
- *Ephesians 2:10* — "We are His workmanship."

Summary of Truths

- Inherited lies create cycles; Kingdom truth creates freedom.
- You are not bound to repeat what you were taught.
- Comparison is a counterfeit mirror.
- Gratitude restores perspective.

- God calls you His workmanship—complete, intentional, and enough.

CHAPTER 5

"THE BURDEN BENEATH THE BELLY." PART ONE

Theme & Focus

To the world, a heavy belly may look like evidence of indulgence.In truth, it often carries the invisible weight of living—years of unspoken grief, responsibility, loss, and survival.This chapter opens the door to understanding how emotional and spiritual pressure can settle in the body, and how God invites us to release it through His rest.

The Unseen Load

Many people live under burdens that cannot be measured on a scale.

The "fat belly" becomes a silent journal, recording every disappointment and fear we never dared to voice.

Every sigh we swallowed.

Every "I'm fine" we forced.

Every expectation we tried to carry for everyone else.

When Jesus said,

"Come to Me, all you who are weary and heavy-laden, and I will give you rest" (*Matthew 11:28*),

He was not only speaking to those bent from physical labor; He was speaking to those weighed down by invisible obligations.

We often mistake endurance for holiness and exhaustion for obedience.

The burden beneath the belly is not fat—it is the accumulation of unresolved responsibility.

It is what happens when the soul tries to do God's job.

When Survival Becomes a System

From childhood, we learn to cope: be strong, be quiet, be perfect.

Each unhealed moment becomes stored energy.

The nervous system, built to protect, begins to hold instead of release.

Our ancestors called it "keeping it all inside."

Scripture calls it carrying a yoke that was never ours.

In *Isaiah 46:4*, God says,

"I will carry you; I will sustain you, and I will rescue you."

But many believers reverse that promise—they try to carry God's work, sustain everyone else, and rescue themselves.

When the soul lives in constant defense, the body compensates.

The abdomen—the center of breath and strength—tightens and stores stress.

What looks like physical heaviness may actually be spiritual armor.

Kingdom Insight

The Kingdom truth is simple yet radical:

You were never designed to carry what Christ already bore.

At Calvary, Jesus took on both sin and sorrow (*Isaiah 53:4*).

He did not only remove guilt; He absorbed grief.

Every tear you internalized, every apology you made for existing, was part of the burden He lifted.

Still, many live as if redemption is a loan to repay instead of a gift to receive.

They hold onto guilt because letting go feels like neglecting responsibility.

But grace is not irresponsibility—it is divine permission to stop self-punishment.

The Voice of the Weight

If your body could speak, what would it say?

For many, it would whisper, "I'm tired of holding this."

The body remembers everything the mouth refused to confess.

This is why God calls confession a pathway to healing (*James 5:16*).

Confession is not merely verbal; it is physical—it releases tension from the heart into the hands of mercy.

When we suppress pain, we feed shame.

When we express truth, we feed faith.

The burden beneath the belly is the cry of a spirit longing to exhale.

Spiritual Application – Step 1: Recognize the Pattern

1. **Notice when you tighten.**Moments of criticism, stress, or fear often trigger the body's defensive posture.
2. **Name what you feel.**Say, "Lord, right now I feel unseen," or "I feel responsible for too much."
3. **Invite God into the moment.**Whisper, "You carry this better than I do."

Each recognition loosens the internal knot.

Release begins not through effort, but through permission—permission to let God be God.

Closing Reflection

The belly does not only digest food; it digests life. When overloaded, it swells with what the heart cannot process. But healing begins when we exchange holding for handing over.

Psalm 55:22 says,

"Cast your burden on the Lord, and He will sustain you."

The invitation is constant:

Lay it down.

Let Him lift it.

Let the body breathe again.

CHAPTER 5

"THE BURDEN BENEATH THE BELLY." PART TWO

Carrying the Weight of Expectations

There is a kind of heaviness that creeps in slowly—the weight of being needed.It begins as duty and matures into depletion.We take on expectations that were never assigned to us: to be the strong one, the peacemaker, the provider, the one who never breaks.

Society has taught many, especially women of faith, to equate service with self-erasure.

But even Jesus, who carried the cross, paused under its weight. Simon of Cyrene was commanded to help Him (*Luke 23:26*).

If the Son of God accepted assistance, why do we treat help as weakness?

God never asked His daughters and sons to prove strength by carrying alone.

He asked them to abide, not to accumulate.

When you live in chronic self-reliance, the soul learns to brace itself.

The body responds as if every day were an emergency—muscles tightening, breath shortening, the stomach guarding. That is how spiritual strain becomes physical weight.

When the Body Keeps the Score

Science affirms what Scripture revealed first: the body records memory.

Unreleased grief becomes fatigue.

Suppressed fear becomes inflammation.

Unspoken guilt becomes heaviness in the core.

David wrote,

"When I kept silent, my bones wasted away through my groaning all day long." — *Psalm 32:3*

He described what modern psychology now calls embodied stress.

God designed confession, prayer, and praise not as rituals, but as release valves.

Each act of worship is a divine exhale—your body's way of agreeing with freedom.

When you lift your hands, you loosen your shoulders.

When you sing, you expand your lungs.

When you weep, you cleanse the soul's mirror.

This is not emotional weakness; it is spiritual alignment.

Kingdom Insight

Freedom does not come by shrinking the body; it comes by lightening the soul.

Many pray for weight loss when what they truly need is burden loss.

The Holy Spirit's work is not cosmetic—it is catalytic.

He changes what you carry by changing how you think.

Romans 12:2 commands:

"Be transformed by the renewing of your mind."

Renewal begins with rest.

When you stop fighting yourself, your body stops fighting for control.

The Spirit brings rhythm where there was resistance.

The same hands that shaped the earth now shape peace within you.

Spiritual Application – Step 2: Practice Release

1. **Daily Surrender:** At the end of each day, name one thing you carried that was not yours and verbally hand it to God.

2. **Physical Symbol:** Stretch, breathe, or walk slowly while repeating, "I cast my cares on You."

3. **Renewed Confession:** Replace every "I must fix it" with "He is faithful."

Each repetition re-educates the nervous system to trust divine order.

When Rest Feels Foreign

Rest can feel uncomfortable for those who have survived chaos.

Stillness threatens the ego that believes control equals safety.

Yet the Lord whispers,

"In returning and rest you shall be saved; in quietness and confidence shall be your strength." — *Isaiah 30:15*

Learning to rest is not laziness; it is obedience.

It is the refusal to let anxiety finish what grace already completed.

Take note: the enemy hates rest because rest proves faith.

When you are still, you declare, "God is enough."

The belly softens, the breath lengthens, and worship becomes easier.

Closing Reflection

The burden beneath the belly was never only about food or appearance.

It was about what you thought you had to carry to be loved.

But the cross of Christ redefines love—it is not earned; it is received.

Lay down every invisible load: the memory of failure, the pressure to perform, the fear of letting others down.

Hear Jesus speak again,

"My yoke is easy, and My burden is light." — *Matthew 11:30*

He was not exaggerating.

When you exchange your burden for His, even your posture changes—spirit upright, shoulders lifted, soul breathing again.

Freedom begins when you believe you were never meant to be the Savior.

You were meant to be saved.

Key Scriptures

- *Matthew 11:28–30* — "Come to Me... My yoke is easy and My burden is light."
- *Psalm 55:22* — "Cast your burden on the Lord, and He will sustain you."
- *Isaiah 30:15* — "In returning and rest you shall be saved."
- *Romans 12:2* — "Be transformed by the renewing of your mind."

Summary of Truths

- Physical heaviness often hides spiritual exhaustion.
- God never called you to carry what Christ already bore.
- Confession, worship, and rest are divine tools of release.
- The body is not your enemy; it is a messenger inviting you to surrender.
- Freedom comes by exchanging striving for stillness.

CHAPTER 6

WHEN THE HEART FEELS HEAVY - PART ONE

Theme & Focus

Every heart carries weights that the world cannot see.This chapter opens the door to understanding how emotional and spiritual heaviness settles deep within—and how God's presence begins to lift it.A heavy heart is not weakness; it is a signal that the soul needs rest in its Maker.

The Hidden Weight of a Weary Soul

We often measure weariness by what our hands do, but the heaviest work happens inside the chest.

It is the quiet labor of holding disappointment, fear, and the memory of words that bruised the spirit.

A person can smile and still be burdened.

They can pray faithfully and still feel dull inside, as if the light has dimmed.

This is the weight of an over-responsible heart—one that tries to fix everything God never asked it to fix.

King David knew this fatigue when he cried,

"My heart is sore pained within me... fearfulness and trembling are come upon me." — *Psalm 55:4–5*

He longed to flee from the storm of his own emotions, yet God met him not with escape, but with endurance.

A heavy heart is not abandoned—it is invited to exchange burdens.

When Compassion Turns into Carrying

Many hearts become heavy through compassion without boundaries.

We take on the pain of others until empathy turns into exhaustion.

We say yes when the Spirit whispered no, afraid that resting might look selfish.

But Jesus Himself withdrew to lonely places to pray (*Luke 5:16*).

Even the Healer paused to be held by the Father.

If the Son of God needed sacred pauses, then so do we.

When compassion is led by guilt instead of grace, the heart fills with a subtle resentment that sounds like fatigue.

God never called us to carry—He called us to care under His direction.

Kingdom Insight

Heaviness is often the result of accumulated care without consistent casting.

Peter's instruction was not poetic—it was practical:

"Cast all your care upon Him, for He cares for you." — *1 Peter 5:7*

To cast means to throw, not to hand over politely.

God invites a complete release, not quiet endurance.

The Kingdom life is not weightless; it is well-distributed.

When you carry what belongs to you—obedience, stewardship, faith—you walk in peace.

When you carry what belongs to God—control, outcomes, fear—you walk in pressure.

When Silence Speaks Louder Than Words

Heaviness thrives in silence.

Unspoken grief grows roots, tightening around the joy that once flowed freely.

Many believers were taught that lament shows a lack of faith, but Scripture proves otherwise:

"Pour out your heart before Him; God is a refuge for us." — *Psalm 62:8*

Lament is not complaining; it is holy honesty.

It tells God the truth about where you are so He can reveal the truth about who He is.

Each time you release sorrow in prayer, the heart regains rhythm.

The Lord trades silence for song.

Spiritual Application – Step 1: Identify the Load

1. **Name it:** Write down what has been occupying your thoughts when you lie awake.
2. **Locate it:** Ask the Holy Spirit, "Where did I pick this up? Was it mine to carry?"
3. **Lift it:** Speak aloud, "Lord, I give You this concern. I trust You with what I cannot change."

Do this daily until it becomes instinctive.

This practice doesn't ignore pain; it places pain where healing happens.

Closing Reflection

A heavy heart is not a broken one; it is a burdened one.

The same heart that feels too full of sorrow can also overflow with peace once it remembers who truly holds it.

God is not asking you to harden your heart—He is asking you to hand it over.

When you do, heaviness begins to lift, and love flows freely again.

Key Scriptures

- *Psalm 55:22* — "Cast your burden on the Lord, and He will sustain you."
- *1 Peter 5:7* — "Cast all your care upon Him, for He cares for you."
- *Psalm 62:8* — "Pour out your heart before Him."

CHAPTER 6

WHEN THE HEART FEELS HEAVY - PART -TWO

The Weariness of Waiting

Some of the deepest heart-heaviness doesn't come from trauma but from time—the long delay between prayer and promise.Waiting tests faith like nothing else.

When answers seem silent, the mind begins to question: *Did I hear God correctly? Am I still worthy of His attention?*

This emotional ache is subtle but draining. It lingers in the heart as restlessness and in the body as tension.

Abraham and Sarah knew this pain. Their waiting stretched across decades, yet the covenant never changed. God's delay was not denial; it was development.

Faith matures in waiting.

Hope is refined when sight is withheld.

The heavy heart must remember that delayed manifestation does not mean divine neglect.

Carrying Guilt and Self-Blame

Another form of heaviness comes from guilt—either for what we've done or what we failed to do.

When unresolved, guilt becomes the heart's chain. It whispers, *You should have known better.*

But guilt, when redeemed, becomes guidance.

Conviction from the Holy Spirit always points forward; accusation always points backward.

That's why Paul could say,

"Forgetting what is behind and straining toward what is ahead." — Philippians 3:13

God never shames us into change.

He draws us into transformation.

When you accept forgiveness, you are not ignoring your past—you are agreeing with grace.

When the Heart Hardens to Protect Itself

A wounded heart often builds walls disguised as wisdom.

We call it "discernment," but sometimes it's simply fear in camouflage.

We avoid vulnerability to avoid pain, but the same walls that keep out hurt also block healing.

Proverbs 4:23 teaches,

"Guard your heart, for everything you do flows from it."

Guarding is not closing; it is filtering—keeping truth in and lies out.

A guarded heart stays soft toward God even when it is cautious toward the world.

Ask yourself: *Have I built walls or boundaries?*

Walls trap. Boundaries teach freedom with peace.

Kingdom Insight

Heaviness is often the heart's cry for renewal.

It is God's indicator light, reminding you that love and trust need replenishing.

The Kingdom operates through rhythm—work and worship, sowing and rest, giving and receiving.

When we live outside that rhythm, the heart begins to protest through heaviness.

Jesus modeled that rhythm perfectly. He ministered to the multitudes, then withdrew to solitary places.

He poured out and then refilled.

The heavy heart is healed when it learns to do the same—to breathe in grace after every exhale of service.

Isaiah 40:31 promises,

"They that wait upon the Lord shall renew their strength."

Renewal is not instant; it is continual.

The Spirit doesn't remove all weight—He replaces it with worship.

Spiritual Application – Step 2: Release and Receive

1. **Pray honestly:** Tell God exactly what feels heavy. Use your own words.

2. **Visualize the exchange:** Picture placing that weight into His hands and receiving His peace.
3. **Rest intentionally:** Take one act of rest today—a walk, silence, or deep breathing—without guilt.
4. **Repeat renewal:** Each day, renew your strength through gratitude and Scripture.

The goal is not to be weightless but to be well-carried.

Closing Reflection

When the heart feels heavy, remember: God never designed you to live without help.

The Holy Spirit is called the Helper because He lifts what you cannot.

Let this truth settle deeply—

You are not failing when you are tired; you are simply forgetting to lean.

In the Kingdom, the measure of strength is not how much you hold but how quickly you hand it over.

When you yield, Heaven yields strength.

"Come to Me," Jesus still says, "and you will find rest for your souls." — Matthew 11:29

That rest is not temporary relief; it is restoration. When the heart rests, the whole body follows.

Key Scriptures

- **Philippians 3:13** – "Forgetting what is behind and straining toward what is ahead."

• **Proverbs 4:23** – "Guard your heart, for everything you do flows from it."

• **Isaiah 40:31** – "They that wait upon the Lord shall renew their strength."

• **Matthew 11:29** – "You will find rest for your souls."

Summary of Truths

- Waiting and guilt are major sources of heaviness.
- The enemy uses delay to plant doubt; God uses it to produce depth.
- Grace replaces guilt; worship replaces weariness.
- Softness of heart is strength, not weakness.
- True renewal happens through rhythm—pour out, then refill.

CHAPTER 7

BREAKING THE CURSE OF CONDEMNATION-PART-1

Theme & Focus

Condemnation Is the Shadow That Follows Shame

It speaks in the tone of religion but not the voice of God. This chapter begins the work of exposing how condemnation masquerades as conviction—and how the finished work of Christ has already broken its curse.

When Guilt Becomes a Prison

Guilt has a purpose—it alerts the conscience when we've stepped outside divine order.

But when guilt remains after forgiveness, it mutates into condemnation, becoming a prison without bars.

The heart begins to replay mistakes as proof of identity: *I failed, therefore I am a failure.*

That lie is the enemy's favorite strategy because it keeps believers forgiven yet still bound.

Paul confronted this deception directly:

"There is therefore now no condemnation for those who are in Christ Jesus." — Romans 8:1

Condemnation keeps you living under a verdict that Heaven has already overturned.

How the Curse Works

A curse is a word that empowers failure and prevents flourishing.

Condemnation functions the same way—it curses your confidence and convinces you that God tolerates you instead of treasures you.

It disguises itself as humility, saying, *I'm just being honest about my flaws.*

But self-criticism is not humility—it is agreement with accusation.

The spirit of condemnation doesn't always shout; sometimes it whispers:

You'll never get it right.

If people knew who you really were...

These quiet condemnations are spiritual toxins.

They drain faith, hinder prayer, and silence worship.

The moment you begin to internalize those words, the curse gains legal ground.

That is why Jesus, hanging on the cross, declared,

"It is finished." — John 19:30

He was breaking every spoken and unspoken judgment that would ever stand against you.

Kingdom Insight

Conviction and condemnation are opposites dressed in similar clothing.

Conviction	**Condemnation**
Comes from the Holy Spirit	Comes from the accuser
Points to grace and change	Points to guilt and shame
Lifts the heart	Lowers the soul
Leads to repentance	Leads to retreat
Ends in freedom	Ends in fear

The Holy Spirit convicts to restore relationship; the enemy condemns to destroy confidence.

Both speak to the conscience, but only one leads you home.

The Emotional Weight of Condemnation

Condemnation doesn't live only in the mind; it seeps into the body.

It tightens the chest, shortens the breath, and keeps the shoulders bent.

It creates a posture of punishment—always waiting for something to go wrong.

This constant readiness for rejection exhausts the heart. But the Kingdom invites you to stand upright—not in arrogance, but in adoption.

Romans 8:15 reminds us,

"You have received the Spirit of adoption, by whom we cry, 'Abba, Father!'"

Adoption nullifies accusation.

When you know who your Father is, no other verdict can define you.

Spiritual Application – Step 1: Recognize the False Verdict

1. **Listen to the tone of your thoughts.**Does it accuse or invite? Condemnation scolds; conviction beckons.
2. **Ask the Spirit for evidence.**If the guilt has no remedy but despair, it's not from God.
3. **Replace the ruling.**Speak aloud: "The case against me is closed by the blood of Jesus."

Each declaration lifts another layer of false judgment from the soul.

Closing Reflection

Condemnation feeds on silence and secrecy.

It dies when exposed to the light of truth.

The curse cannot continue where confession and grace are present.

You do not owe God perpetual penance for forgiven sins. He does not keep receipts for what the cross already covered.

Freedom begins when you stop rehearsing guilt and start rehearsing gratitude.

The blood of Jesus is not a temporary pardon—it is a permanent acquittal.

Key Scriptures

- **Romans 8:1** – "There is therefore now no condemnation for those who are in Christ Jesus."
- **John 19:30** – "It is finished."
- **Romans 8:15** – "You have received the Spirit of adoption."

CHAPTER 7

BREAKING THE CURSE OF CONDEMNATION-PART-2 LIVING BEYOND THE VERDICT

Freedom Is Not Just the Removal of Guilt—It Is the Restoration of Joy

Many believers receive forgiveness but still live like parolees, afraid of returning to spiritual prison. They check their record daily instead of celebrating their release.

But in the Kingdom, there is no probation—only pardon.

The blood of Jesus does not grant temporary access; it grants eternal belonging.

Your name was written in Heaven's registry, not penciled in.

Hebrews 10:22 invites us to approach God with a clean conscience:

"Let us draw near with a sincere heart in full assurance of faith, having our hearts sprinkled clean from an evil conscience."

An *evil conscience* is not one that sins—it is one that keeps accusing after being forgiven.

The curse of condemnation breaks the moment you accept this truth: God is not angry with you; He is inviting you closer.

The Cycle of Self-Punishment

Condemnation keeps people trapped in cycles of self-punishment—fasting to earn love, overworking to feel valuable, hiding when they stumble.

This is not holiness; it is bondage wearing a halo.

You cannot crucify yourself enough to improve the cross.

The sacrifice has already been made.

Your repentance was never meant to replace grace—it was meant to reveal it.

Every time you rehearse guilt, you reopen wounds that Jesus already sealed.

To live condemned is to keep mourning what Heaven has already buried.

Romans 8:33 asks,

"Who shall bring a charge against God's elect? It is God who justifies."

The answer is clear: no one—not even you.

Kingdom Insight

Condemnation thrives when we measure holiness by perfection.

But Kingdom holiness is not flawlessness—it is alignment.

It is returning again and again to the One who makes you whole.

Grace is not an excuse; it is an escort.

It takes you out of judgment and walks you into freedom.

This is why the enemy hates grace—it cannot be earned or revoked.

When you truly believe grace, condemnation loses its audience.

John 3:17 declares,

"For God did not send His Son into the world to condemn the world, but to save the world through Him."

If Jesus didn't come to condemn, then condemnation has no legal right to remain.

Walking in Kingdom Liberty

To live beyond condemnation is to live in agreement with grace.

You will still make mistakes, but repentance becomes a moment of restoration, not a marathon of shame.

When you fall, the Spirit lifts you—not to remind you of failure but to reintroduce you to freedom.

Psalm 34:5 says,

"They looked to Him and were radiant, and their faces were not ashamed."

Notice the order—first they looked, then they shone.

Condemnation breaks when your gaze shifts from self to Savior.

Radiance is the evidence of redemption.

Spiritual Application – Step 2: Walk in Your Acquittal

1. **Renew your confession daily:** Say aloud, "I am justified by faith and covered by grace."
2. **Reject rehearsed regret:** Stop narrating old failures. Each repetition reopens a lie.
3. **Rehearse radiance:** Each time shame speaks, lift your chin and remember—He has already spoken your name in mercy.

The proof of grace is peace. When your heart quiets, you know the curse is broken.

Closing Reflection

Condemnation is a parasite—it cannot survive without your agreement.

When you stop feeding it guilt, it starves.

The Father's love is not on trial—only your willingness to believe it is.

Stand tall under the verdict of grace.

You are no longer under judgment; you are under Jesus.

Every chain of self-punishment has been melted by mercy.

Walk out of the courtroom of accusation and into the temple of acceptance.

The Judge has become your Defender.

Key Scriptures

- **Hebrews 10:22** — "Let us draw near with a sincere heart in full assurance of faith."

- **Romans 8:33** — "Who shall bring a charge against God's elect? It is God who justifies."
- **John 3:17** — "God did not send His Son to condemn the world."
- **Psalm 34:5** — "They looked to Him and were radiant, nd their faces were not ashamed."

Summary of Truths

- Condemnation imitates conviction but produces fear, not freedom.
- You cannot out-repent grace—you can only receive it.
- Holiness is alignment, not perfection.
- Grace is the courtroom where judgment turns into joy.
- You are justified, radiant, and free.

CHAPTER 8

THE MIRROR OF MERCY - PART 1

Theme & Focus

The mirror does not lie—but it also does not love. What it shows is real, but not always true. This chapter begins the transformation from self-evaluation to divine revelation, teaching us how to see the reflection God sees—not a body of imperfection, but a vessel of mercy.

The First Look

Every day begins with a reflection.

Some people glance quickly; others linger. But for many, the mirror has become an altar of judgment.

It does not ask questions—it delivers verdicts.

Its glass repeats the same message shame once whispered: "You are not enough."

But mercy interrupts that ritual.

When you stand before the mirror in God's light, the reflection changes—not because your face does, but because your faith does.

Mercy reframes the image.

Where the world sees wrinkles, mercy sees wisdom.

Where the world sees scars, mercy sees stories.

Where the world sees excess, mercy sees evidence—you survived.

The Mirror as a Messenger

In the Kingdom, mirrors are not meant to condemn but to confirm identity.

James 1:23–25 warns that those who hear the Word but do not act on it are "like a man observing his natural face in a mirror... and immediately forgets what kind of man he was."

The problem is not the mirror; it's the memory.

The physical mirror reflects appearance, but the Word reflects essence.

When you look into Scripture and believe it, you are not just reading—you are remembering.

Mercy acts as the bridge between what you see and what God said.

Without mercy, the mirror is harsh; with mercy, it becomes holy.

When Reflection Becomes Rejection

Condemnation begins where mercy is absent.

Many believers confuse self-awareness with self-attack.

They think humility means agreeing with their worst critic.

But humility is not thinking less of yourself—it is thinking of yourself through God's truth.

To reject what God calls beautiful is not humility; it is rebellion against His design.

When you reject yourself, you reject the reflection of His image.

Genesis 1:27 declares,

"So God created man in His own image; in the image of God He created him."

Every time you curse your reflection, Heaven hears it as blasphemy against creation.

That is how serious God is about mercy—He insists that you see yourself through it.

Kingdom Insight

Mercy does not deny imperfection; it redefines it.

To live in mercy is to walk in continual forgiveness—of self, of others, of yesterday.

Mercy is not weak; it is weightless. It removes what guilt tries to glue to your soul.

When God looks at you, He sees you through Christ, not through comparison.

You are not measured against other believers—you are measured by grace.

The mirror of mercy reflects your becoming, not your before.

Lamentations 3:22–23 reminds us,

"His mercies are new every morning."

This means every sunrise carries permission to start over.

The same face you thought unworthy yesterday becomes sacred today because mercy renewed the view.

Spiritual Application – Step 1: Look Again

1. **Stand before your mirror in silence.** Instead of criticizing, breathe and ask, "Lord, show me what You see."
2. **Speak mercy aloud.** Replace every negative thought with a declaration of truth: "I am fearfully and wonderfully made." (Psalm 139:14)
3. **Smile with gratitude.** Not because of perfection, but because of presence—He is in you.

You will know mercy has taken root when your reflection no longer starts an argument but begins a conversation with God.

Closing Reflection

Mercy changes mirrors.

It turns judgment into joy and regret into remembrance.

It allows you to look at yourself without flinching, because you finally see what Heaven has been seeing all along.

The goal of faith is not to escape your reflection—it is to align it.

Mercy is the lens that lets you see holiness within humanity.

Key Scriptures

- James 1:23–25 — The mirror of the Word reflects true identity.
- Genesis 1:27 — You are made in the image of God.

- Lamentations 3:22–23 — His mercies are new every morning.
- Psalm 139:14 — “I am fearfully and wonderfully made.”

CHAPTER 8

THE MIRROR OF MERCY - PART 2

Living Through the Lens of Grace

The mirror of mercy does not merely change what you see; it changes how you live. When you begin to look at yourself through grace, your actions start to align with that vision.

Behavior follows belief—so when you believe you are beloved, you begin to live as beloved.

Many spend their days trying to fix what mercy has already forgiven.

They chase approval through performance, believing transformation begins with effort.

But Kingdom renewal begins with acceptance—not of sin, but of sonship.

You cannot reflect God's image while rejecting His affection.

Mercy invites you to stop editing your identity and start embodying His intention.

From Mirror to Window

As mercy matures, the mirror becomes a window.

You no longer look only at yourself; you look through yourself to see God's glory shining within.

Paul wrote,

"We all, with unveiled faces, contemplate the Lord's glory and are being transformed into His image with ever-increasing glory." — 2 Corinthians 3:18

The unveiled face is a face unashamed.

When Moses came down from the mountain, his face shone with reflected light, yet he veiled it to hide the fading.

Christ removes that veil in us—no more hiding, no more retending.

Mercy makes the heart transparent so that others can see Christ, not self-consciousness.

Kingdom Insight

The mirror of mercy functions like the altar of worship—it requires honesty and intimacy.

Every time you approach it, you reaffirm that your worth is rooted in who you are, not in what you weigh or how you appear.

The enemy uses mirrors to accuse; the Spirit uses them to affirm.

When you truly see through mercy's lens, you can minister from healed places instead of hiding them.

Your scars become sermons; your weakness becomes witness.

You no longer need to cover the belly of shame because you've discovered the beauty of burden turned into testimony.

Mercy doesn't erase history—it redeems it.

Spiritual Application – Step 2: Practice Seeing Differently

1. **Morning Mercy Ritual:** Each morning, look into the mirror and thank God for one attribute that reflects His work in you.
2. **Evening Reflection:** Before bed, look again and ask, "Lord, where did I show mercy today?"
3. **Speak the Blessing:** Place your hand on your heart and say, "This body houses Your Spirit; may it reflect Your glory."

Over time, the mirror becomes an altar of agreement—where your perception joins Heaven's proclamation: "It is good."

The Transformation of Vision

True healing happens when you stop seeing mercy as a moment and begin seeing it as your mode of vision.

You start interpreting life through redemption instead of regret.

Even failure becomes feedback, not finality.

To see through mercy is to see from God's perspective—never blind to flaws, but never bound by them either.

It is freedom that keeps teaching you how to love without limits.

When you embrace mercy's reflection, you no longer live self-aware; you live Spirit-aware.

You begin walking as a mirror of God's mercy to others.

Closing Reflection

Mercy's mirror doesn't show a perfect image; it shows a progressing one.

Every day, you see a little more of who you are in Him and who He is in you.

The goal is not to escape reflection but to let your reflection preach.

When others look at you and see peace instead of pretense, they encounter the mercy that has made its home in you.

The mirror no longer defines you—it reminds you.

You are forgiven.

You are favored.

You are free.

Key Scriptures

• 2 Corinthians 3:18 — "We all... are being transformed into His image."

• Romans 5:20 — "Where sin increased, grace abounded much more."

• Psalm 103:11–12 — "As far as the east is from the west, so far has He removed our transgressions."

Summary of Truths

- Mercy transforms self-judgment into self-acceptance.
- The mirror is no longer an enemy but an altar.
- Grace shifts focus from fixing to reflecting.
- True transformation happens through continual vision, not occasional effort.
- You were created to reflect God's mercy to the world.

CHAPTER 9

"THE LANGUAGE OF HEALING - PART ONE

Theme & Focus

Words are not merely sounds—they are spiritual seeds. They build, break, bind, and bless. Every word released carries either life or limitation. This chapter begins the journey of reclaiming your language so that what leaves your lips agrees with Heaven's decree, not shame's narrative.

The Power Hidden in Speech

In the beginning, God created with words:

"And God said... and it was so." — Genesis 1

Before there was form, there was sound.

Before there was healing, there was a declaration.

Creation did not begin with movement—it began with speech.

Because we are made in His image, our words share that same creative nature.

When we speak, we build environments.

When we murmur, we invite decay.

Every sentence is a seed that eventually produces fruit—either peace or poison.

Proverbs 18:21 says,

"Death and life are in the power of the tongue, and those who love it will eat its fruit."

The question is not whether you are eating your words—it's what kind of harvest they're producing.

When Words Wound

Many people live under the echo of words spoken decades ago.

A single sentence—"You're too much," "You'll never change," "You're not enough"—can plant roots that reach deep into adulthood.

These verbal scars don't just remain in memory; they shape identity.

They alter posture, self-belief, even appetite.

What others once spoke over you, you may now speak over yourself.

Shame often uses the mouth as its microphone.

It makes you narrate your life from a place of fear rather than faith.

The most damaging lies are not the ones others told you, but the ones you began telling yourself.

The Internal Dialogue

Your inner voice is the echo of your beliefs.

If it's filled with criticism, it's likely repeating old condemnation.

If it's filled with compassion, it's reflecting Kingdom alignment.

Healing begins when you interrupt that inner conversation—when you stop asking, "What's wrong with me?" and start declaring, "God is still working in me."

Paul wrote,

"Let no corrupt communication proceed out of your mouth, but only what is good for building up." — Ephesians 4:29

This includes the conversations you have with yourself.

The same grace you offer others must also be offered inwardly.

Otherwise, your own words will work against your prayers.

Kingdom Insight

In the Kingdom, healing travels on the breath of truth.

That's why confession and proclamation are powerful—they realign your atmosphere.

Jesus healed through words: "Be clean." "Rise and walk." "Peace, be still."

Each phrase was not a suggestion—it was spiritual legislation.

Your mouth is a ministry tool.

It can either magnify wounds or manifest wellness.

To speak healing, you must believe that your words matter.

Faith must fill your vocabulary.

When you declare what God declares, Heaven's authority echoes through earthly air.

Spiritual Application – Step 1: Audit Your Atmosphere

1. **Listen to your language.** What do you say when you're tired, frustrated, or afraid?
2. **Identify contradictions.** Do your declarations match your prayers—or do they cancel them?
3. **Replace reaction with revelation.** When negativity rises, respond with Scripture instead of silence.

Each correction reshapes your internal climate until faith becomes your first response.

Closing Reflection

Healing begins with the tongue.

Every word you speak either stitches or splits the soul.

To heal the heart, you must heal your habits of speech.

Begin to speak as one who believes that God's Word in your mouth carries the same power it held in His—because it does.

Speak gently.

Speak truthfully.

Speak life—because life is listening.

Key Scriptures

- **Genesis 1:3** — "And God said... and it was so."
- **Proverbs 18:21** — "Death and life are in the power of the tongue."
- **Ephesians 4:29** — "Let no corrupt communication proceed out of your mouth."

CHAPTER 9

THE LANGUAGE OF HEALING – PART TWO

The Vocabulary of Wholeness

Healing requires a new dialect. You cannot speak the language of bondage and expect the fruit of freedom. Many believers sabotage their deliverance by speaking in contradictions:

"I'm healed, but I still feel broken."

"I'm blessed, but nothing ever works out."

Your words must grow into agreement with God's Word.

The mouth is not a thermometer that reports circumstances—it is a thermostat that sets them.

Isaiah 57:19 reveals God's design:

"I create the fruit of the lips: Peace, peace to those who are far and near."

God doesn't just answer prayer; He creates through confession.

When your lips speak life, Heaven partners with your declaration.

How Healing Sounds

Healing has a sound.

It's not loud; it's consistent.

It doesn't demand attention; it draws it.

The healed person begins to sound like faith—calm under pressure, gentle under provocation, grateful under trial.

This sound is not denial; it is dominion.

It speaks from victory, not for it.

You don't declare healing to persuade God; you declare it to remind yourself of what He's already done.

When Jesus said to the paralyzed man, "Rise, take up your bed, and walk," He spoke possibility into paralysis.

Your healing begins the same way—when you start calling movement into what has been still.

Kingdom Insight

Your words not only describe your world—they design it.

That's why the adversary attacks speech.

If he can infect your confession, he can redirect your destiny.

In Numbers 13, the Israelites called themselves grasshoppers, and they became what they confessed.

Their words framed fear as fact.

But Joshua and Caleb spoke differently; they said, "We are well able."

They inherited what they declared.

The Kingdom principle is clear:

- What you believe shapes your thoughts.
- What you think shapes your words.
- What you speak shapes your world.

To change your world, change your words.

To change your words, change what you believe about yourself in Christ.

The Language of Prayer

Prayer is Heaven's classroom for vocabulary.

In prayer, you learn the tone of trust.

When your words begin to align with God's Word, you start praying from identity, not insecurity.

Instead of begging, you begin to bless.

Instead of rehearsing lack, you release gratitude.

You start declaring, "Lord, I thank You that healing is already working in me."

This shift releases divine peace, even before physical manifestation appears.

Peace is often the first symptom of answered prayer.

Spiritual Application – Step 2: Speak Life Daily

1. **Morning Declarations:** Begin each day with three affirmations grounded in Scripture. Example:

- "I walk in divine health."

- "My words build, not break."
- "The joy of the Lord is my strength."

2. **Midday Mindfulness:** Pause halfway through the day to check your speech. Ask, "Have my words agreed with faith or fear today?"
3. **Evening Recalibration:** Before sleep, thank God for every opportunity to speak life, and ask forgiveness for words that wounded.

Over time, you'll notice that the more you guard your words, the lighter your heart becomes.

Healing begins to echo through your entire being.

The Sound of Agreement

When Heaven and Earth speak the same thing, miracles manifest.

Healing accelerates when your confession becomes cooperation.

That's why the enemy prefers silence—he knows your silence can stall your deliverance.

But every time you open your mouth to bless, even while broken, you declare war on shame.

You remind the unseen realm that your voice still belongs to God.

Psalm 107:20 declares,

"He sent His Word and healed them."

When that same Word comes out of your mouth, healing flows through your life.

Closing Reflection

Every healing begins with a conversation.

God spoke, and the universe aligned.

You speak, and your world realigns.

Let your words become worship

Let your sentences become songs of surrender.

Let every conversation carry the fragrance of faith.

For when your speech sounds like Heaven, your life starts to look like it.

Key Scriptures

- **Isaiah 57:19** — "I create the fruit of the lips."
- **Numbers 13:33 / 14:9** — "We are well able to overcome it."
- **Psalm 107:20** — "He sent His Word and healed them."
- **Proverbs 18:21** — "Death and life are in the power of the tongue."

Summary of Truths

- Healing requires a language of agreement, not anxiety.
- Your words design your environment.
- Confession is not a ritual; it's a creative act.
- Silence delays what speech can deliver.

- Speak life until life speaks back.

CHAPTER 10

THE SPIRIT OF RESTORATION – PART TWO

Restoration Beyond Repair

The Holy Spirit does not merely fix what is broken—He recreates what was lost. Restoration is Heaven's signature on what the enemy tried to erase. It's not God patching the old; it's Him planting the new.

Joel 2:25 records one of the most astonishing promises in Scripture:

"I will restore to you the years that the locust has eaten."

Notice—it doesn't say *days* or *things*; it says *years.*

God restores time.

Only His Spirit can reclaim seasons you thought were wasted and turn them into testimonies that accelerate your purpose.

Every lost opportunity, every quiet *almost,* every unfulfilled dream still has a destiny under divine reconstruction.

Restoration is not delayed—it's being delivered in stages, like a sunrise rising over your life one beam at a time.

Restoration of Relationships

The Spirit not only heals the inner man but also reconciles the outer world.

Many people long for restoration but resist reconciliation because it feels vulnerable.

But when God restores, He often rebuilds connection first—He mends the bridges shame burned.

He does not erase boundaries; He renews compassion.

Forgiveness becomes the foundation on which restoration stands.

Ephesians 4:32 reminds us,

"Be kind and compassionate to one another, forgiving each other, just as in Christ God forgave you."

Forgiveness is not approval; it is release.

It removes the weight of carrying another person's offense.

It reopens the heart to joy, which shame had closed.

As you forgive, you make space for the Spirit to restore what bitterness had blocked.

Kingdom Insight

The Spirit of Restoration is both architect and artist.

He rebuilds structure and renews beauty.

He restores discipline to the mind and delight to the soul.

Isaiah 61:3 declares that the Spirit gives *"beauty for ashes, joy for mourning, and praise for the spirit of heaviness."*

That exchange is the essence of Kingdom restoration.

Ashes represent what once burned—dreams, relationships, hopes.

Beauty is not a replacement for ashes; it is what rises from them.

God never wastes pain; He recycles it into power.

What you call *ruin*, He calls *resource.*

The rubble becomes revelation; the debris becomes design.

The Spirit takes every piece and turns it into part of the masterpiece.

The Restoration of Identity

The greatest miracle of restoration is remembering who you are.

Sin distorts identity; shame disguises it.

But the Spirit restores the believer's awareness of divine sonship.

Romans 8:16 proclaims,

"The Spirit Himself testifies with our spirit that we are children of God."

That testimony silences accusation.

When you know whose you are, you stop competing for worth.

Restoration reinstates you as an heir, not a hireling.

You are not returning to the outer courts—you are being escorted back to the throne room of relationship.

Spiritual Application – Step 2: Partner with the Process

1. **Pray for restoration, not repetition.** Ask God to build better, not just bring back.
2. **Speak the language of gratitude.** Thank Him for what's being restored, even before it's visible.
3. **Align your actions with renewal.** Live as though restoration has already happened; it will follow faith's footsteps.

Restoration is sustained through cooperation.

The Spirit works where willingness abides.

The Rhythm of Restoration

True restoration happens in rhythm—release, receive, rebuild.

You cannot rebuild what you refuse to release.

You cannot receive while holding resentment.

The Spirit leads you step by step until peace feels permanent and confidence feels holy again.

As you walk this journey, remember that restoration doesn't erase history—it redeems it.

Every testimony of pain becomes a portal of ministry.

What once embarrassed you will soon empower others.

Closing Reflection

The Spirit of Restoration is moving even now—quietly, faithfully, powerfully.

He's turning your sighs into songs, your ruins into revelation, your fatigue into fire.

Let the words of Isaiah 58:12 anchor your heart:

"You will be called the Repairer of the Breach, the Restorer of Streets to Dwell In."

This is your inheritance—to become what was done for you.

You were restored to restore.

You were healed to heal.

You were renewed to reveal.

And through it all, the Spirit whispers, *"I am making all things new."*

Key Scriptures

- **Joel 2:25** — "I will restore the years the locust has eaten."
- **Ephesians 4:32** — "Forgive each other, just as God forgave you."
- **Isaiah 61:3** — "Beauty for ashes, joy for mourning."
- **Romans 8:16** — "The Spirit testifies that we are children of God."
- **Isaiah 58:12** — "You will be called the Restorer of the Breach."

Summary of Truths

- Restoration is divine re-creation, not repair.
- The Spirit rebuilds relationships and identity simultaneously.
- Forgiveness clears the space where restoration grows.
- God restores both time and testimony.
- You are not just restored—you are commissioned as a restorer.

CHAPTER 10

THE SPIRIT OF RESTORATION – PART ONE

Theme & Focus

Restoration is the language of Heaven. Where shame destroys, grace rebuilds. Where guilt depletes, the Holy Spirit breathes again. This chapter opens with the divine promise that no matter how fractured a person's soul may feel, God's Spirit has both the will and the power to restore it completely.

The Nature of Restoration

Restoration is not repair—it is re-creation.

Repair fixes what was; restoration returns it to what God intended.

It does not merely restore function—it restores fellowship, dignity, and divine rhythm.

Psalm 23:3 declares:

"He restores my soul; He leads me in the paths of righteousness for His name's sake."

The phrase *"He restores"* means to cause to return—to bring back something that has wandered too far or broken too deeply.

The Spirit's first ministry to the weary is not correction—it is comfort.

He begins the work of making whole what the world said was too damaged to matter.

When Shame Scatters and the Spirit Gathers

Shame always scatters—it divides identity, isolates the soul, and fractures confidence.

Restoration, however, does the opposite: it gathers.

It collects every fragment and weaves them back into a testimony.

In Luke 15, Jesus spoke of the shepherd leaving ninety-nine sheep to find the one that was lost.

That image reveals God's restorative heart—He refuses to let any part of you stay missing.

Even when your confidence is lost in the wilderness of comparison, He calls it by name and carries it home.

The Spirit of Restoration specializes in unfinished stories.

He finds the unspoken, heals the unseen, and redeems the unremembered.

You do not have to return to where you broke; He brings healing where you are.

The Breath of Renewal

The Spirit restores not by effort, but by breath.

Genesis 2:7 says that God "breathed into man's nostrils the breath of life."

That same breath still moves through every believer today—the breath of renewal.

When you exhale disappointment and inhale faith, you participate in a divine exchange.

Breath becomes prayer, and prayer becomes healing.

This is why the Holy Spirit is called the Comforter, not the critic.
He does not accuse; He awakens.

He whispers, "You are not finished; you are being formed."

Restoration is not a moment—it is a movement.

Each breath of surrender becomes a brick in the rebuilding of your peace.

Kingdom Insight

The Spirit of Restoration moves wherever faith creates room.

He restores through remembrance—reminding you of who you are in Christ.

John 14:26 says:

"The Helper, the Holy Spirit... will teach you all things and bring to your remembrance all that I have said to you."

That remembrance is more than mental recall—it is spiritual realignment.

Each truth He brings back to memory rebuilds what falsehood tried to erode.

He restores through revelation:

- What shame hid, He unveils.
- What fear locked, He unlocks.
- What sorrow drained, He refills.

You may not recognize yourself after restoration—and that is the point.

God doesn't want to return you to who you were before the pain; He wants to reveal who you were always meant to be.

Spiritual Application – Step 1: Make Room for Renewal

1. Quiet the noise. Turn off external voices long enough to hear the whisper of the Spirit.
2. Breathe intentionally. Each inhale is an invitation; each exhale is release.
3. Invite the Spirit to rebuild. Say aloud: "Holy Spirit, restore what I surrendered to shame."

This is not imagination—it is participation in the process of divine healing.

The Spirit rebuilds what the heart permits.

Closing Reflection

The Spirit of Restoration is always near, never hurried, and endlessly gentle.

He waits for your "yes" to begin the rebuilding.

Every time you choose hope over hiding, you hand Him another stone for your new foundation.

You are not being pieced back together; you are being reborn into purpose.

Every scar, every silence, every setback becomes part of your restored design.

Let this truth echo in your soul:

What shame dismantled, grace will resurrect.

Key Scriptures

- Psalm 23:3 — "He restores my soul."
- Luke 15:4–6 — The shepherd gathers the lost.
- Genesis 2:7 — The breath of life renews creation.
- John 14:26 — "The Helper... will bring to remembrance all I have said to you."

CHAPTER 11

BREAKING EMOTIONAL AGREEMENTS WITH SHAME – PART ONE

Theme & Focus

Some wounds heal on the surface while still bleeding beneath.Every unhealed emotion eventually seeks agreement—an inner contract that says, *"This is who I am now."* This chapter begins the work of exposing those silent covenants made with shame and replacing them with the eternal covenant of grace.

What Is an Emotional Agreement?

An emotional agreement is a belief your heart signs without your conscious permission.

It often begins in pain—a rejection, a harsh word, a betrayal, or a repeated failure.

Somewhere deep within, the soul whispers, *"Maybe they're right about me."*

That whisper becomes a signature.

It's not written on paper—it's written on perception.

It governs how you see yourself, how you speak, and how you respond to love.

It's the quiet *"yes"* that binds you to lies that were never meant to live inside you.

These emotional contracts give shame legal ground in your thought life.

They authorize condemnation to sit where confidence should reign.

But through the Spirit of truth, those agreements can be revoked—permanently.

How Shame Demands Agreement

Shame is not content to visit—it seeks residence.

It feeds on repetition; every time you rehearse an old failure or compare yourself to someone else, you renew the lease.

It insists on participation—it wants your voice to echo its accusations.

When you agree with shame, even unintentionally, it reshapes your identity.

It whispers:

- "I am broken beyond repair."
- "I'm too late for purpose."
- "God forgave me, but I can't forgive myself."

Each statement becomes a small covenant with pain. But the moment you begin to disagree—when you speak the truth of who God says you are—the contract starts to crumble.

Kingdom Insight

Emotional agreements are spiritual bonds that can only be broken by truth and authority.

The enemy cannot maintain what revelation exposes.

John 8:32 declares,

"You shall know the truth, and the truth shall make you free."

Freedom begins with awareness.

You cannot break what you have not named.

Once you identify the lie you've lived under, the Holy Spirit helps you replace it with divine truth.

For every false belief, there is a scriptural truth waiting to evict it:

Lie	Truth
"I am unworthy."	"You are accepted in the Beloved." — Ephesians 1:6
"I am a failure."	"You are more than a conqueror." — Romans 8:37
"I'm forgotten."	"I have inscribed you on the palms of My hands." — Isaiah 49:16

The more you speak truth, the weaker the lie becomes.

Recognizing the Signs of Agreement

You may have made emotional agreements without realizing it if:

- You apologize for existing.
- You feel unqualified to receive love or blessing.
- You shrink in moments that call for confidence.
- You rehearse your past more than your promises.

These are symptoms of spiritual bondage disguised as humility.

But God is calling His people to cancel what shame has written and to sign new declarations of life.

Breaking the Agreement

The process of breaking emotional agreements is both spiritual and intentional.

You must engage your will and your words.

Start by identifying the root.

Ask the Holy Spirit, *"When did I start believing that lie?"*

He will show you the moment—sometimes through memory, sometimes through emotion.

Then speak this aloud:

"I renounce every agreement I made with shame, fear, and unworthiness.

I cancel every lie that contradicts the truth of who I am in Christ.

I receive the mind of Christ and the freedom of His Spirit."

This is not ritual; it is repentance in its purest form—a returning to truth.

Spiritual Application – Step 1: Identify and Renounce

1. **Write the lie.** Name the false belief that has guided your emotions.
2. **Find the truth.** Locate a Kingdom scripture that directly refutes it.
3. **Speak the exchange.** Say aloud: "I release this lie and receive truth."
4. **Seal it with worship.** Lift praise where shame once sat—it seals the freedom.

Every declaration creates distance between your spirit and shame's influence.

Soon, the voice that once accused you will fade beneath the roar of grace.

Closing Reflection

Emotional freedom begins when you decide that your feelings will no longer be your foundation—truth will.

The soul that once agreed with shame begins to echo Heaven's affirmation instead:

"I am chosen. I am redeemed. I am whole."

You are not bound by your history; you are held by His holiness.

The same Spirit that raised Christ from the dead is rewriting your emotional agreements line by line.

The ink of shame fades where the blood of Jesus is applied.

Key Scriptures

- John 8:32 — "You shall know the truth, and the truth shall make you free."
- Ephesians 1:6 — "Accepted in the Beloved."
- Romans 8:37 — "More than conquerors through Him who loved us."
- Isaiah 49:16 — "I have inscribed you on the palms of My hands."

CHAPTER 11

BREAKING EMOTIONAL AGREEMENTS WITH SHAME – PART TWO

Restoring the Inner Covenant

Once false emotional agreements are broken, the heart must sign a new covenant—one rooted in truth, grace, and divine belonging.Deliverance without replacement leaves empty space; restoration fills it with new identity. God never removes without restoring.

Ezekiel 36:26 promises,

"I will give you a new heart and put a new spirit within you."

The new heart doesn't just feel differently—it believes differently.

Where you once agreed with lies, you now align with love.

That is the work of the Spirit of Restoration in your emotions: turning your inner courtroom into a sanctuary of peace.

From Shame to Covenant Confidence

Every believer must understand the difference between agreement and alignment:

- **Agreement** accepts what was said about you.
- **Alignment** accepts what God says of you.

The moment you agree with divine truth, spiritual gravity shifts.

You begin to think and speak like Heaven.

Condemnation loses its vocabulary because your confession now carries Kingdom authority.

Hebrews 10:16 declares,

"I will put My laws into their hearts, and in their minds I will write them."

The Spirit writes over every erased identity with divine affirmation.

No longer "I am not enough," but "I am more than enough through Christ."

No longer "I am alone," but "I am indwelt by His presence."

This is covenant confidence—the assurance that shame has no jurisdiction over your redeemed emotions.

Kingdom Insight

Breaking emotional agreements is not the end; it's the beginning of emotional stewardship.

You must now protect what was restored.

Every healed heart needs boundaries built from truth.

The enemy will test your freedom by offering old thoughts wrapped in new disguises.

But discernment grows sharper after deliverance.

You'll recognize his tone because it no longer matches your Father's.

Philippians 4:8 becomes your boundary verse:

"Whatever is true, whatever is honorable, whatever is right... think on these things."

That command is not just about positivity—it's about protection.

It keeps your emotional agreements rooted in righteousness.

Rebuilding the Inner Dialogue

Your inner dialogue must now mirror God's dialogue.

To rebuild your emotions is to re-educate your language.

What you say inwardly becomes what you feel outwardly.

Begin each morning by blessing your soul:

"Soul, remember who you are. You are beloved, not broken. You are purposed, not punished."

David practiced this often. In Psalm 42:11, he spoke directly to himself:

"Why are you cast down, O my soul? Hope in God!"

Self-talk becomes spiritual talk when it agrees with Scripture.

Each declaration is an act of healing—training your emotions to follow faith instead of fear.

Spiritual Application - Step 2: Establish New Emotional Agreements

1. **Renew Daily:** Write one truth each day that directly contradicts a lie you once believed.

2. **Guard Gently:** When shame resurfaces, do not argue—affirm truth. Simply say, "That's not my agreement anymore."

3. **Celebrate Growth:** Every time peace replaces panic, gratitude replaces guilt, or joy returns after sorrow, you're witnessing evidence of new emotional contracts with God's Word.

Emotional restoration is not perfection—it is progress sanctified by presence.

The Power of Divine Agreement

Heaven responds to agreement.

When your emotions, mind, and spirit harmonize with God's Word, miracles manifest naturally.

You begin to live in rhythm with divine will.

Matthew 18:19 says,

"If two of you agree on earth concerning anything they ask, it will be done by My Father in Heaven."

When your heart and your faith agree, you form that same partnership—Heaven and humanity in concert. Restoration becomes not just something God does for you, but something He does through you.

Closing Reflection

Shame once demanded your consent, but grace now invites your cooperation.

Every agreement with fear has been torn, and a new covenant signed in peace stands in its place.

The Spirit whispers, *"Your signature is no longer on sorrow; it's on sonship."*

You belong to truth now.

Every time you choose love over loathing, peace over panic, and faith over fear, you renew that divine agreement.

Walk in it daily—free, favored, and firmly established in Kingdom identity.

Key Scriptures

- Ezekiel 36:26 — "I will give you a new heart and put a new spirit within you."
- Hebrews 10:16 — "I will put My laws into their hearts and write them on their minds."
- Philippians 4:8 — "Think on these things."
- Psalm 42:11 — "Why are you cast down, O my soul? Hope in God."
- Matthew 18:19 — "If two agree on earth... it will be done."

Summary of Truths

- Emotional agreements are broken by revelation and replaced by restoration.

- The Spirit writes truth where shame once ruled.
- Boundaries of peace protect new emotional freedom.
- Inner speech must echo divine truth to sustain healing.
- You now live under covenant confidence, not condemnation.

CHAPTER 12

THE WEIGHT OF WORDS UNSPOKEN - PART ONE

Theme & Focus

Silence has a sound. It hums beneath the surface of unspoken pain, hidden disappointment, and unexpressed truth.This chapter reveals that what is left unsaid does not disappear—it settles. Unspoken words become spiritual weight, pressing on the heart until the Spirit invites them into light and healing.

When Silence Becomes a Burden

Many carry memories they've never named, hurts they've never voiced, and questions they've never dared to ask.

At first, silence feels safe—it keeps the peace, avoids conflict, and hides vulnerability.

But over time, silence hardens into a second skin.

It isolates the soul, creating invisible walls between you and the world around you.

David described this inward ache vividly in Psalm 32:3: "When I kept silent, my bones wasted away through my groaning all day long."

Silence suppresses not only words but wellness.

The longer pain remains unspoken, the more it occupies spiritual space.

Your unspoken story becomes an unhealed story—and the enemy thrives in what you withhold from God.

The Spiritual Cost of Suppression

Silence does not sanctify suffering—it extends it.

When pain is not expressed, it often mutates into something heavier: bitterness, exhaustion, or self-doubt.

Unspoken emotions begin to interpret life through old wounds instead of present grace.

You may find yourself thinking:

- "It's easier to say nothing than to risk being misunderstood."
- "If I speak, they won't believe me."
- "My feelings don't matter."

Each of these thoughts acts like a stone in the heart. Over time, the soul becomes burdened—not by the weight of circumstance, but by the weight of words that were never released.

Kingdom Insight

The Kingdom principle of healing is expression through truth.

God heals what is revealed.

The first step to freedom is not perfection—it's permission: permission to speak, to weep, to remember, to name what hurts.

Jesus modeled this transparency in Gethsemane when He said,

"My soul is overwhelmed with sorrow to the point of death." — *Matthew 26:38*

If the Son of God could speak His sorrow aloud, then silence should never be mistaken for strength.

God invites honesty, not performance.

Your voice was designed for worship and warfare—not withdrawal.

When the Spirit leads you to speak, it's not to expose weakness but to expose what weakens you.

The Healing Power of Voice

The tongue that once cursed can now heal.

Proverbs 12:18 says,

"The tongue of the wise brings healing."

Speaking is more than communication—it is creation.

When you speak your truth to God, you give Him material to work with.

Your voice becomes the instrument through which the Holy Spirit orchestrates freedom.

Words unspoken are like prayers unsent—they never reach their destination.

But the moment you speak truth, even through tears, Heaven responds.

Your sound summons strength.

Spiritual Application – Step 1: Break the Silence

1. **Speak to God First:** Begin by confessing your unspoken hurts in prayer. Whisper them, write them, or cry them out—He listens in every language.

2. **Share with Safety:** Ask the Spirit to reveal trustworthy spaces and people who can hold your story without judgment.

3. **Replace Fear with Faith:** Every time you share your truth, declare, "I release this weight into the hands of grace."

Breaking silence is not rebellion—it's restoration.

Your voice is the key that unlocks your healing.

Closing Reflection

The silence that once protected you is now restricting you.

God is calling you to open your mouth so He can open your heart.

What you release, He redeems.

Every unsaid word surrendered to Him becomes seed for restoration.

Remember: Heaven never heals what we hide, but always redeems what we reveal.

Let this be the day you begin to speak again.

Key Scriptures

- *Psalm 32:3* — "When I kept silent, my bones wasted away."

- *Matthew 26:38* — "My soul is overwhelmed with sorrow."
- *Proverbs 12:18* — "The tongue of the wise brings healing."

CHAPTER 12

THE WEIGHT OF WORDS UNSPOKEN - PART TWO

The Voice That Heals

When God restores your voice, He restores your vision. Every word spoken in truth clears the fog that silence once created.What was buried under the weight of unspoken pain becomes the soil where boldness begins to grow.

Your voice is not fragile—it is forged.

It carries the sound of survival, the resonance of one who endured, believed, and rose again.

Psalm 107:2 declares,

"Let the redeemed of the Lord say so, whom He has redeemed from the hand of the enemy."

To "say so" is to reclaim authority.

Every testimony you speak aloud becomes a weapon against shame and a bridge for someone else's deliverance.

You are not only speaking for yourself—you are speaking for those still silent.

When Expression Becomes Deliverance

Many try to heal in silence, yet true breakthrough rarely happens without sound.

God's design for freedom is participatory—you must speak your way out.

In the natural, sound waves move matter.

In the spiritual, truth moves mountains.

When Jesus stood before Lazarus's tomb, He cried with a loud voice, "Lazarus, come forth!"

The miracle followed the command.

Every word of truth you release carries that same resurrection power.

Speaking breaks spiritual inertia.

It releases energy, invites empathy, and establishes reality.

When you speak what once shamed you, the enemy loses leverage—because secrecy is his strategy, but speech is your salvation.

Kingdom Insight

The sound of confession creates space for transformation.

Confession is not humiliation—it is liberation.

To confess means "to agree with."

When you confess truth, you are agreeing with God's perspective, not your pain's perception.

Romans 10:10 affirms,

"With the heart one believes unto righteousness, and with the mouth confession is made unto salvation."

Healing must move from belief to broadcast—from heart to mouth.

Belief saves the soul; confession frees the body.

That's why worship feels lighter than worry—worship speaks what faith already knows.

The Ministry of Conversation

Conversation is sacred ground.

When you open your heart in dialogue—with God, with a trusted friend, or within a safe community—you allow the Holy Spirit to minister through presence.

Healing happens in honest spaces.

James 5:16 gives us the blueprint:

"Confess your faults one to another, and pray for one another, that you may be healed."

Notice the connection between confession and healing.

When words flow, wounds close.

Conversation becomes communion, and empathy becomes evidence of the Spirit's work.

You don't need eloquence—you need authenticity.

God anoints ordinary exchanges filled with extraordinary honesty.

Spiritual Application – Step 2: Transform Silence into Sound

1. **Speak the Truth in Prayer:** Begin each day by voicing one truth about your journey to God. Example: "Lord, I'm still healing, but I thank You that I'm no longer hiding."

2. **Testify Publicly:** When the Spirit prompts you, share your testimony with someone who needs it. Every story you tell builds faith in another.

3. **Worship Out Loud:** Sing, pray, and declare Scripture audibly. The sound of your voice reinforces what your spirit already knows.

Over time, these practices will turn your once-silent places into sanctuaries of sound. Your voice will become the echo of God's restoration in motion.

The Sound of Freedom

Freedom is not quiet—it resounds.

It laughs again, prays again, and praises without permission.

The same mouth that once rehearsed sorrow now rehearses strength.

Isaiah 42:10 commands,

"Sing to the Lord a new song, and His praise from the ends of the earth."

Every new song begins with a healed heart.

When you finally sing again, even softly, you announce to the world—and to every spirit of shame—that you are no longer bound by silence.

Your melody becomes your mantle.

Your voice becomes your victory.

Closing Reflection

Silence once felt safe, but now your safety is found in sound.

You were never meant to carry pain quietly—you were meant to cast it through confession.

The Father delights in your voice; Heaven recognizes its tone.

Every word you speak in faith fills the atmosphere with light.

The weight of unspoken words has been lifted, replaced by the rhythm of restoration.

You are free to speak, to sing, and to testify—because your voice now belongs to victory.

Key Scriptures

- *Psalm 107:2* — "Let the redeemed of the Lord say so."
- *John 11:43* — "Lazarus, come forth!"
- *Romans 10:10* — "With the mouth confession is made unto salvation."
- *James 5:16* — "Confess your faults… and pray for one another."
- *Isaiah 42:10* — "Sing to the Lord a new song."

Summary of Truths

- Silence conceals, but speech heals.
- Your voice carries resurrection power.
- Confession aligns you with Heaven's truth.

- Conversation is ministry; authenticity invites anointing.
- Every sound of praise proclaims freedom over your life.

CHAPTER 13

RECLAIMING THE TEMPLE WITHIN - PART ONE

Theme & Focus

The body is not a burden—it is a temple. It was never designed to carry guilt, exhaustion, or neglect, but to house glory. This chapter begins the restoration of physical reverence—an invitation to reclaim your body as a sacred dwelling place of the Spirit, worthy of care, honor, and peace.

The Temple and the Presence

From the beginning, God's presence has always desired a place to dwell.

In the wilderness, it was a tabernacle. In Jerusalem, it was a temple. And now—in the believer—it is you.

Paul wrote in **1 Corinthians 6:19–20:**

"Do you not know that your body is a temple of the Holy Spirit within you, whom you have from God? You are not your own; you were bought with a price."

The temple is not only spiritual—it is also physical.

Your hands are meant for healing, your voice for blessing, your mind for meditation, and your body for worship.

Every act of care is an act of reverence.

When you treat your body with honor, you declare to Heaven and to hell alike that you understand your value.

How Shame Distorts Stewardship

Shame convinces believers that the body is an enemy to be controlled rather than a vessel to be cherished.

For many, "fat-belly shame" has become not just an image issue but a spiritual identity issue.

The body, instead of being celebrated as the workmanship of God, becomes a constant reminder of comparison and criticism.

But God never called the temple ugly—He called it holy.

When He said in **Leviticus 20:26,**

"You shall be holy to Me, for I the Lord am holy,"

He meant *wholly*—every part, every cell, every structure dedicated to His purpose.

To despise your body is to disagree with your Designer.

To neglect your health is to silence your instrument of worship.

The first step in reclaiming the temple is repentance—not only for overeating or under-resting, but for believing the lie that your worth is measured by appearance instead of assignment.

The Spirit of Reverent Care

- Reverence for the body begins with awareness:
- Awareness that rest is worship.

- Awareness that nourishment is obedience.
- Awareness that movement is praise.

Romans 12:1 urges,

"Present your bodies as a living sacrifice, holy and acceptable to God—this is your reasonable service."

This presentation is not about punishment; it's about partnership.

You cooperate with the Spirit by offering Him a vessel capable of sustaining His work.

Self-care, under Kingdom authority, becomes sacred discipline.

When you drink water with gratitude, you are acknowledging the Living Water.

When you walk in peace, you are moving the feet of Christ in the earth.

When you rest, you mirror the God who rested on the seventh day.

Kingdom Insight

The temple must be cleansed before it can be filled.

In **John 2:15–16,** Jesus drove out the merchants who had turned the temple into a marketplace.

Likewise, the Spirit drives out every thought, habit, and indulgence that desecrates His dwelling.

Cleansing is not condemnation—it is consecration.

The Lord is not shaming you; He is shaping you.

He removes clutter so that glory has room to dwell.

Your body does not need perfection to be holy—it needs permission to be healed.

Holiness is not the absence of flaw but the presence of function.

When every part of you begins to serve purpose again, restoration is complete.

Spiritual Application – Step 1: Honor Your Sanctuary

1. **Bless your body aloud.** Say: "This is God's temple. It is fearfully and wonderfully made."
2. **Listen to your body's language.** Fatigue, hunger, and pain are invitations to pause, not punish.
3. **Create a rhythm of rest and reverence.** Schedule Sabbath moments—time to breathe, reflect, and release tension.

Each action retrains the soul to treat the body as beloved property of the King.

Closing Reflection

The Spirit of God lives within you—not abstractly, but actually.

He moves through your breath, your heartbeat, your steps.

Every time you choose rest over resentment, nourishment over neglect, gratitude over guilt—you are rebuilding His temple, stone by stone.

This is not vanity; it is victory.

The shame that once mocked your form has lost its license.

You are the dwelling place of glory—and it is time to live like it.

Key Scriptures

- **1 Corinthians 6:19–20** — Your body is the temple of the Holy Spirit.
- **Leviticus 20:26** — "You shall be holy to Me."
- **Romans 12:1** — "Present your bodies as a living sacrifice."
- **John 2:15–16** — Jesus cleansed the temple.

CHAPTER 13

RECLAIMING THE TEMPLE WITHIN - PART TWO

The Discipline o Divine Maintenance

Reclaiming the temple is not a single act—it is a lifelong rhythm of reverence. Restoration without maintenance eventually leads back to ruin. The Holy Spirit restores your body as His dwelling, but you must partner with Him to keep it consecrated.

1 Corinthians 9:27 reminds us,

"I discipline my body and bring it under control, so that after preaching to others I myself will not be disqualified."

Paul understood that discipline is not punishment; it is preservation.

Your body cannot carry divine assignment if it is constantly depleted, ignored, or misused.

Stewardship is worship.

Every act of care—drinking water, walking in peace, sleeping when you need rest—is a declaration that your temple still matters to God.

The Rhythm of Rest and Renewal

God built rest into creation.

After six days of forming the heavens and the earth, He rested—not from exhaustion, but from completion.

That same rest remains holy today.

Rest does not mean inactivity; it means intentional recovery.

The temple cannot host glory on an empty tank.

When you pause to restore your strength, you honor the rhythm of Heaven.

Isaiah 30:15 says,

"In returning and rest you shall be saved; in quietness and confidence shall be your strength."

Rest is not weakness—it is wisdom.

When you practice rest, you proclaim that God, not striving, sustains your life.

Nourishment as an Act of Worship

The foods you choose, the way you eat, and even the gratitude in your heart are all spiritual expressions.

The table is an altar; the meal is a reminder that God still provides.

Eating with awareness invites the Spirit into the simplest moments of life.

When you nourish your body, do it prayerfully:

"Lord, thank You for this provision. Let this meal strengthen me to serve You well."

The temple cannot burn pure incense if the lamp is starving for oil.

Likewise, your spirit burns brightest when your body is cared for in love, not guilt.

Kingdom Insight

The enemy attacks the temple subtly—not through destruction, but through distraction.

He keeps believers busy, fatigued, and disconnected from their rhythm of peace.

But the Spirit teaches a different pace—the pace of purpose.

Jesus never hurried, yet He was never late.

He ministered from overflow, not exhaustion.

That same rhythm is available to you.

To reclaim your temple is to reclaim your pace—walking with the Spirit, not racing against time.

Galatians 5:25 declares,

"If we live by the Spirit, let us also walk in the Spirit."

Walking implies steady movement—intentional, peaceful, and guided by divine timing.

The Temple and Emotional Detox

Physical restoration cannot thrive where emotional toxins still linger.

The temple must be cleansed both inside and out.

Release resentment.

Forgive yourself.

Let your tears become cleansing waters.

Psalm 51:10 says,

"Create in me a clean heart, O God, and renew a right spirit within me."

Forgiveness is not forgetting—it is freeing.

Every release opens new space for the Spirit's presence.

As your emotions detox, your body begins to follow—stress lifts, breath deepens, and peace settles.

Holiness feels lighter than heaviness.

Spiritual Application – Step 2: Practice Whole-Body Worship

1. **Morning Consecration:** Upon waking, touch your heart and declare, "This temple belongs to the Lord."
2. **Midday Renewal:** Take a few minutes each day to stretch, breathe, and invite the Spirit to refresh you.
3. **Evening Reflection:** Thank God for how your body served Him that day—every task, every word, every moment of rest.

These simple acts retrain the soul to honor God in both flesh and faith.

The Reward of Reverence

When you reclaim the temple, you reclaim clarity.

You hear God more clearly because the noise of neglect is gone.

Peace takes residence where pressure once ruled.

The Spirit delights to dwell in order.

Where there is reverence, there is revelation.

As you maintain your temple, your body becomes a broadcast of His glory.

Isaiah 58:11 promises,

"The Lord will guide you continually, satisfy your soul in drought, and strengthen your bones."

Strengthened bones, strong foundation, steady purpose—that is the mark of a temple truly reclaimed.

Closing Reflection

The temple within is not made of stone but of surrender.

Every time you honor your body with gratitude, you build another altar of praise.

The Spirit's presence fills the space you make for Him.

Breathe deeply.

Rest intentionally.

Walk reverently.

For this temple—your temple—belongs wholly to God.

Key Scriptures

- Corinthians 9:27 — Discipline preserves divine purpose.
- Isaiah 30:15 — "In rest and quietness is your strength."
- Galatians 5:25 — "Walk in the Spirit."
- Psalm 51:10 — "Create in me a clean heart."
- Isaiah 58:11 — "He will strengthen your bones."

Summary of Truths

- Discipline protects what deliverance restores.
- Rest is a holy rhythm, not a luxury.
- Nourishment and self-care are forms of worship.
- The Spirit walks, not races, with the believer.
- A cleansed heart strengthens a consecrated body.

CHAPTER 14

LEARNING TO LIVE LIGHT: THE FREEDOM OF RELEASE – PART ONE

Theme & Focus

To live light is to live liberated. This chapter opens the path of release—learning to surrender the weights of worry, regret, perfection, and people-pleasing. Heaven never intended for you to carry what grace has already covered. Release is not losing—it is making room for glory.

The Invitation to Lay It Down

Jesus said,

"Come to Me, all who labor and are heavy-laden, and I will give you rest." — *Matthew 11:28*

The word *labor* means to strive under strain; *heavy-laden* means loaded beyond design.

When you carry more than you were created for, even blessings can begin to feel like burdens.

Living light begins with accepting Christ's invitation—not to perform, but to pause.

The Savior's first gift to the weary soul is permission:

"You may stop striving now."

Release is trust in action.

It says, *"I believe God is big enough to hold what I'm letting go."*

The Burden of Control

Much of our weight is invisible—it hides in the urge to manage outcomes, fix people, and predict tomorrow.

Control masquerades as strength, but it is rooted in fear.

When we grip too tightly, peace slips through our fingers.

Proverbs 3:5–6 teaches,

"Trust in the Lord with all your heart and lean not on your own understanding; in all your ways acknowledge Him, and He will make your paths straight."

Trust is the exchange rate of the Kingdom.

Every time you surrender control, Heaven deposits clarity.

The lighter you live, the farther you see.

Unpacking Emotional Luggage

The spirit of heaviness often hides in the suitcase of the soul—stuffed with disappointment, unforgiveness, comparison, and guilt.

We keep carrying old narratives because we fear who we'd be without them.

But the Kingdom calls us to travel light:

"Lay aside every weight, and the sin which so easily ensnares us." — *Hebrews 12:1*

Weights are not always wicked—they're simply unnecessary.

Some relationships, routines, and thoughts were meant for a season, not a lifetime.

To release them is not betrayal; it's obedience.

The Lord does not ask you to discard people but to disentangle from the pressures that pull you away from peace.

Kingdom Insight

Release is the rhythm of renewal.

Even creation lives by this pattern—trees drop leaves, rivers release water, hearts exhale forgiveness.

Holding on may feel safe, but it delays new growth.

When you release, you make space for replacement.

God cannot fill closed hands.

Open hands become altars, and open hearts become vessels.

Psalm 55:22 affirms,

"Cast your burden on the Lord, and He shall sustain you."

Casting is not gentle—it's decisive.

Throw it, don't toss it.

The force of surrender brings the peace of stillness.

Spiritual Application – Step 1: Identify Your Weights

1. **List the Loads.** Write down what currently feels heavy—responsibilities, memories, expectations, or fears.

2. **Label the Source.** Ask yourself, "Did God give me this, or did I pick it up?"
3. **Loosen the Grip.** Pray aloud: *"Lord, I release what You never required and embrace what remains."*

Each release shifts the soul closer to equilibrium—where peace becomes your natural posture.

Closing Reflection

Living light is not careless living; it is *care-free* living—a life unburdened by shame, hurry, or the need for human approval. To live light is to walk in rhythm with grace, breathing at Heaven's pace. Every burden you surrender becomes a testimony that God's strength is enough.

Remember: You were never created to carry everything—only to carry His presence.

The rest must be released.

Key Scriptures

- *Matthew 11:28* — "Come to Me… and I will give you rest."
- *Proverbs 3:5–6* — "Trust in the Lord… and He will make your paths straight."
- *Hebrews 12:1* — "Lay aside every weight."
- *Psalm 55:22* — "Cast your burden on the Lord."

CHAPTER 14

LEARNING TO LIVE LIGHT: THE FREEDOM OF RELEASE – PART TWO

The Rhythm of Daily Release

Release is not a one-time act; it's a spiritual rhythm. Each day brings new weights disguised as responsibilities, expectations, and emotions. The mature believer learns to practice continual unloading—to let go before life becomes heavy again.

Lamentations 3:23 reminds us,

"His mercies are new every morning; great is Your faithfulness."

If mercy renews daily, then release must too.

You were not created to carry yesterday's burdens into today's mercies.

Every morning is an altar of exchange—your worry for His wisdom, your weight for His will.

Living light requires conscious surrender: choosing peace before productivity and presence before pressure.

The Freedom of Simplicity

Complexity clutters the soul. Simplicity is not lack—it is clarity. The more you simplify, the more you sanctify your focus.

Jesus modeled simplicity in both lifestyle and mission.

He traveled light, spoke truth plainly, and kept His attention on the Father's will.

He said in John 5:19,

"The Son can do nothing of Himself, but only what He sees the Father doing."

To live light is to live in sync with Heaven.

When you remove distractions and unnecessary noise, revelation flows freely.

The Spirit cannot fill a schedule that leaves no room for stillness.

Simplify your days until peace fits easily within them.

Letting Joy Do the Lifting

Joy is Heaven's strength training for the soul.

It lifts what gratitude makes light.

Nehemiah 8:10 says,

"The joy of the Lord is your strength."

Joy doesn't ignore difficulty—it outshines it.

To live light is to choose joy as your default emotion, not your reward.

Joy is not the result of everything going right; it's the response to knowing God is right there.

When joy leads, heaviness loses authority.

Laugh again.

Worship again.

Celebrate small victories—each one is a reminder that grace still works.

Kingdom Insight

The posture of light living is open-handed trust.

An open hand gives, receives, and releases freely.

It never clings—it cooperates.

Philippians 4:6–7 gives the formula for lightness:

"Be anxious for nothing, but in everything, by prayer and supplication with thanksgiving, let your requests be made known to God. And the peace of God… will guard your hearts and minds."

Peace guards what prayer releases.

Anxiety thrives on secrecy; peace thrives on surrender.

The moment you hand it to God, the weight begins to lift.

Every worry transferred becomes worship.

Every prayer whispered becomes progress.

Spiritual Application – Step 2: Practice the Light Life

1. **Morning Exhale:** Before starting your day, breathe deeply and say, "Lord, I release everything I cannot control."
2. **Midday Check-In:** Ask yourself, "What am I holding that isn't mine to carry?" Then release it immediately in prayer.
3. **Evening Gratitude:** End your day by listing three things you're thankful for. Gratitude dissolves heaviness faster than complaint ever could.

When practiced daily, these rhythms keep your heart buoyant and your spirit agile.

Walking in the Weightlessness of Faith

Faith was never meant to be heavy.

It carries you because it's anchored in Someone stronger.

The secret of spiritual lightness is dependence—knowing that the One who sustains the universe can surely sustain you.

Isaiah 46:4 declares,

"Even to your old age I am He… I have made you and I will carry you."

To live light is to rest in divine arms.

The burdens you release are now borne by the Everlasting One.

You were never meant to prove strength—only to reveal surrender.

Closing Reflection

Living light is Kingdom living.

It is the art of releasing daily, loving freely, and resting fully.

It's the quiet confidence that God's shoulders are broader than your struggles.

Every moment you choose to release, Heaven responds with renewal.

You are lighter not because life got easier, but because faith grew stronger.

Let your heart say today:

"I will live light, love deeply, and trust completely."

For where there is freedom, there is flight—and where there is flight, there is grace.

Key Scriptures

- Lamentations 3:23 — "His mercies are new every morning."
- John 5:19 — "The Son can do nothing of Himself but what He sees the Father doing."
- Nehemiah 8:10 — "The joy of the Lord is your strength."
- Philippians 4:6–7 — "Be anxious for nothing... and the peace of God will guard you."
- Isaiah 46:4 — "I have made you, and I will carry you."

Summary of Truths

- Living light is a daily decision to release and rest.

- Simplicity sanctifies focus and restores peace.
- Joy lifts the soul where strength once struggled.
- Prayer transfers weight into worship.
- Surrender is strength in motion.

CHAPTER 15

WHEN GOD REDEFINES BEAUTY - PART ONE

Theme & Focus

True beauty is not found in mirrors or measurements; it is found in manifestation. When God redefines beauty, He removes cultural filters and reveals divine design. This chapter invites you to see yourself as Heaven already sees you—radiant, redeemed, and refined by purpose.

The World's Definition vs. Heaven's Design

The world teaches that beauty is a visual competition. It measures worth by appearances, achievements, and approval. But God never called His daughters ornaments—He called them overcomers.

1 Peter 3:3–4 declares: "Your beauty should not come from outward adornment... but from the unfading beauty of a gentle and quiet spirit, which is of great worth in God's sight."

Heaven measures beauty by the radiance of the heart, not the ratio of features.

What the world calls attractive, God calls temporary.

What the Spirit calls beautiful endures forever.

When your heart reflects holiness, you glow with a light no makeup can mimic and no mirror can measure.

The Mirror That Matters

In earlier chapters, we discussed the mirror of mercy; now we see it again—this time as a mirror of identity.

You were made in the image of a beautiful Creator, and His reflection is your reality.

Genesis 1:27 affirms:

"So God created man in His own image… male and female He created them."

To despise your reflection is to insult His workmanship.

Every scar, curve, line, or shade carries a testimony of divine creativity.

God did not craft clones; He designed carriers of His glory.

You are not a random collection of features—you are a living frame for His presence.

Beauty as Holiness Revealed

Holiness beautifies the believer.

Psalm 29:2 says:

"Worship the Lord in the beauty of holiness."

Holiness is not sternness; it is shininess—the soul illuminated by intimacy with God.

When you spend time in His presence, His light settles upon your countenance.

Moses came down from the mountain with his face radiant because he had looked into the eyes of glory.

You cannot encounter divine light and remain dim.

The glow of grace replaces the grime of guilt.

You become living evidence that purity is power.

Kingdom Insight

Kingdom beauty begins with belonging.

When you know you are chosen, comparison dies quietly.

You stop chasing perfection and start embracing purpose.

Ephesians 2:10 declares:

"We are His workmanship, created in Christ Jesus for good works."

The Greek word for "workmanship" is *poiēma*—poem.

You are God's poetry in motion.

Every line of your life is written in rhythm with redemption.

When you finally read yourself through His authorship, beauty becomes effortless.

Divine beauty is not just seen—it's sensed.

It's the peace that follows you, the wisdom that speaks through you, and the compassion that flows from you.

It's what happens when the Spirit within you becomes the glow around you.

Spiritual Application – Step 1: Change Your Lens

1. **Renounce comparison:** Say aloud, "I release every false standard that has defined me."
2. **Reclaim reflection:** Each morning, look into the mirror and declare, "I am God's workmanship, radiant in purpose."
3. **Redefine adornment:** Ask yourself, "Does what I wear represent worth or worry?" Dress as one already approved.

The goal is not to impress, but to express the indwelling glory of God.

Closing Reflection

When God redefines beauty, He does not change your features—He changes your focus.

He invites you to stop critiquing creation and start celebrating craftsmanship.

You are not in need of editing; you are in need of enlightenment.

Holiness has made you luminous.

Every time you worship, forgive, or serve, beauty blooms again.

The more you behold Him, the more beautiful you become.

Key Scriptures

- 1 Peter 3:3–4 — True beauty flows from the spirit.
- Genesis 1:27 — Created in the image of God.

- Psalm 29:2 — "The beauty of holiness."
- Ephesians 2:10 — "We are His workmanship."

CHAPTER 15

WHEN GOD REDEFINES BEAUTY - PART TWO

The Radiance of Reflection

When God redefines beauty, He turns your life into a reflection of His light. The glow that others see is not cosmetics—it's communion. Beauty becomes a byproduct of His presence.

Psalm 34:5 declares,

"They looked to Him and were radiant, and their faces were not ashamed."

Radiance is the evidence of relationship.

Every encounter with God leaves a residue—peace on your countenance, calm in your spirit, confidence in your step.

It's not makeup; it's manifestation.

When people see you, they should see evidence that you've been in the secret place—proof that the temple within has been illuminated by glory.

Confidence Clothed in Grace

The world teaches confidence through comparison.

The Kingdom teaches confidence through communion.

True confidence is not arrogance—it is assurance.

It's knowing who you are and whose you are.

Isaiah 61:10 declares,

"He has clothed me with garments of salvation; He has covered me with the robe of righteousness."

You are already dressed in divine approval.

When you walk in that awareness, you carry quiet authority.

Grace becomes your garment, and peace becomes your posture.

You don't need to demand validation when you're clothed in revelation.

The robe of righteousness fits every believer who refuses to measure themselves by man-made mirrors.

Kingdom Insight

Divine beauty radiates through three qualities: peace, purity, and purpose.

- **Peace** stills the spirit so joy can be seen.
- **Purity** keeps the heart transparent so light can pass through.
- **Purpose** directs the glow so it becomes guidance for others.

You are not called to compete—you are called to complete the reflection of God's image on earth.

When your life shines with compassion, patience, and forgiveness, you become a walking portrait of the Creator's character.

Matthew 5:16 instructs,

"Let your light so shine before others, that they may see your good works and glorify your Father in heaven."

This is Kingdom beauty—light that glorifies, not self-promotes.

The Healing of the Inner Mirror

When the inner mirror is healed, criticism loses its power.

The voices that once spoke inadequacy are replaced with divine affirmation.

You stop asking, "Am I enough?" and start declaring, "God in me is more than enough."

2 Corinthians 3:18 reminds us,"We all, with unveiled faces, beholding the glory of the Lord, are being transformed into the same image from glory to glory."

Transformation is progressive.

Each moment spent beholding Him polishes the mirror of the soul.

You begin to recognize beauty in your process, not just in your perfection.

When your inner dialogue aligns with Heaven's language, you no longer chase validation—you carry it.

Spiritual Application – Step 2: Live the Reflection

1. **Morning Alignment:** Stand before the mirror and speak one truth about your divine beauty. *Example:* "The beauty of the Lord rests upon me."

2. **Midday Grace Check:** When insecurity whispers, answer with the Word: "I am fearfully and wonderfully made."

3. **Evening Illumination:** Reflect on one way God's beauty shone through you today—in patience, kindness, or worship. Record it as testimony of His reflection in your life.

The more you practice reflection, the more radiant your reality becomes.

The Testimony of Transformed Beauty

True beauty testifies.

It speaks without striving, teaches without talking, and draws others toward the light without manipulation. Your story—once marked by shame—is now the stage for His splendor.

Isaiah 61:3 calls this exchange "beauty for ashes."

Ashes are what remain after loss, but beauty is what rises from them. You are living proof that God redeems what life tried to reduce.

Your glow is not vanity; it's victory.

Your reflection is not self-promotion; it's salvation on display.

Closing Reflection

When God redefines beauty, He does not add more color to the outside—He adds more clarity to the inside.

He shifts your gaze from self-consciousness to Spirit-consciousness.

You begin to see yourself as Heaven's masterpiece—holy, radiant, and whole.

Remember: the true mirror of beauty is the face of grace.

And as long as you keep looking at Him, you will never lose your shine.

Key Scriptures

- Psalm 34:5 — "They looked to Him and were radiant."
- Isaiah 61:10 — "He has clothed me with garments of salvation."
- Matthew 5:16 — "Let your light so shine before others."
- 2 Corinthians 3:18 — "Being transformed into His image from glory to glory."
- Isaiah 61:3 — "Beauty for ashes."

Summary of Truths

- True beauty is the reflection of divine presence, not personal performance.
- Confidence grows through communion, not comparison.
- Holiness enhances beauty—it never hides it.
- Each believer becomes a mirror of the Master's light.

- Your glow is your gospel—your peace, the proof of His presence.

CHAPTER 16

THE BENEDICTION OF BECOMING (PART ONE & PART TWO)

Part One – The Journey of Becoming

Becoming is the sacred process between revelation and reflection.It is the space where old identities dissolve and divine ones emerge. Every chapter of your healing has been an unfolding of grace—each layer of shame peeled away to reveal the strength beneath.

The word *becoming* means to come into being, to fit, to adorn.

When God says you are "becoming," He is not merely describing your growth—He is declaring that you are fitting perfectly into His original design.

Philippians 1:6 assures,

"He who began a good work in you will carry it on to completion until the day of Christ Jesus."

The work is not done *to* you—it is done *through* you.

Becoming is not the destination of perfection but the rhythm of transformation.

You are daily being shaped into the likeness of the One who called you.

The Evidence of Transformation

Once, shame spoke louder than purpose.

But now, the whisper of grace has become your new internal sound.

Your story has shifted from "I am broken" to "I am being built."

Where guilt once sat heavy, gratitude now grows.

The same heart that carried insecurity now carries influence.

You no longer hide your humanity—you honor it, for it testifies to divine restoration.

Romans 8:30 declares,

"Those He justified, He also glorified."

Glory is the final garment of the healed.

It's not the applause of people—it's the shine of presence.

Every scar that once symbolized pain now reflects purpose.

Every weakness has become a window for His strength.

Kingdom Insight

The journey of becoming is circular, not linear.

You will return again and again to surrender—but each time with greater wisdom, deeper peace, and stronger faith.

Think of a spiral staircase: each revolution looks the same, yet it rises higher.

Such is the rhythm of your healing—revisiting familiar places from a higher perspective.

This is grace in motion.

Spiritual Application – Step 1: Embrace the Process

1. **Revisit without regret.** Look back only to trace God's fingerprints.
2. **Rest in progress.** Becoming takes time; holiness is built in layers, not leaps.
3. **Rejoice in revelation.** Each insight is another stone in your temple.

You are not behind schedule—you are on divine time.

Closing Reflection (Part One)

Becoming is the benediction of your former self.

It is God's way of saying, "It is finished—but still unfolding."

Every healed moment becomes a hymn.

Every released weight becomes worship.

You are both the temple and the testimony.

CHAPTER 16

PART TWO – THE HEALING LIGHT OF THE HEART

The Image of Transformation

Picture first a person bowed under the invisible shame of the "fat belly." Their shoulders curve inward, their eyes lower, and the light within feels faint.

Around the heart, there is stillness—no movement, no radiant field—just the dull ache of self-criticism and hidden pain.

This is what shame does: it dims the lamp of the heart until divine energy can no longer flow freely.

Now, see what happens when grace enters the atmosphere.

A beam of soft golden light descends—a breath of God moving toward the chest.

It touches the heart, and something shifts.

The heart opens like soil after a long drought, and a pulse of living light begins to expand—first within, then outward in waves.

A gentle field of radiance unfolds, stretching about six feet in every direction, shimmering in hues of gold, sapphire, and pure white.

This is the energy of divine acceptance—the Holy Spirit's flow of love.

It moves through the body, lifting the posture, warming the countenance, and dissolving heaviness.

The "fat belly," once a source of embarrassment, now becomes a symbol of fullness—of life housed in grace.

No longer cursed, it is consecrated.

The person stands upright, the heart shining like a lamp in a crystal vessel.

From this center, waves of peace move outward—six feet and beyond—touching the space around them with stillness and joy.

Within this sphere, shame cannot breathe.

Fear loses its voice.

The body, soul, and spirit align again with divine rhythm.

This is what healing looks like in motion—the heart of flesh restored to its original frequency of love.

Kingdom Insight

The healed heart radiates presence.

It becomes a sanctuary of energy—God's Spirit flowing in, through, and outward.

That radiant six-foot field is more than imagery; it is symbolic of the believer's renewed atmosphere—a zone of peace and purity.

Ezekiel 36:26 proclaims,

"I will give you a new heart and put a new spirit within you."

When that promise becomes reality, the atmosphere changes.

Every person who draws near can feel the warmth of that restoration.

This is the overflow of divine identity—a living aura of grace.

Spiritual Application - Step 2: Activate Your Heart Field

1. **Morning Light Prayer:** Place your hand over your heart and say, "Lord, let Your light flow through me today—cleansing, healing, expanding."

2. **Breath of Renewal:** Inhale slowly, imagining light entering your heart. Exhale shame, fear, and fatigue. Repeat until peace returns.

3. **Extend the Field:** Visualize your heart's glow expanding outward—touching your environment, blessing those around you, and radiating calm strength. You are not absorbing the world's energy—you are projecting Heaven's.

Closing Benediction

May the light of God's Spirit continue to flow through your heart, expanding your field of peace and power.

May every place once wounded by shame now shine with wisdom.

May the fullness that once felt like burden now become your strength and song.

May your countenance glow with grace, your presence carry peace, and your life testify that God still heals from the inside out.

You are whole.

You are radiant.

You are becoming—every day—a clearer reflection of His beauty.

Key Scriptures

- **Philippians 1:6** — "He who began a good work in you will carry it on to completion."
- **Romans 8:30** — "Those He justified, He also glorified."
- **Ezekiel 36:26** — "A new heart will I give you."
- **Psalm 34:5** — "They looked to Him and were radiant."

Summary of Truths

- Becoming is the ongoing work of grace.
- Shame collapses inward; healing expands outward.
- The heart is the divine center of light and life.
- God's energy flows where love is welcomed.
- Your healed presence is your ministry.

Final Word

You have moved from hidden weight to holy light. You are no longer defined by mirrors but by mercy.

Every breath, every heartbeat, every radiance from your soul is proof:

God's Spirit has made His dwelling in you—and He is shining through.

www.ingramcontent.com/pod-product-compliance
Lightning Source LLC
LaVergne TN
LVHW090956080826
845145LV00003B/1025

* 9 7 8 0 9 7 9 2 8 2 1 3 3 *